CW01514158

GEORGIAN COSTUME, TIFLIS

PERSIA:

THE AWAKENING EAST

BY

W. P. CRESSON
F. R. G. S., etc.

WITH ILLUSTRATIONS FROM PHOTOGRAPHS

PHILADELPHIA & LONDON

J. B. LIPPINCOTT COMPANY
1908

TO THE EVER DEAR MEMORY OF
MY MOTHER

421

CONTENTS

ILLUSTRATIONS

9

ILLUSTRATIONS

INTRODUCTION

Since the appearance of Lord Curzon's monumental work on "Persia" it has become almost customary for every new writer dealing with the countries of the Middle East to preface his contribution with an apology for venturing on a field so ably and authoritatively exploited. The author of the present sketch, however, feels that there may still be room for a work dealing in a popular fashion with the present condition of the Shah's empire, and especially with the important events which within the last few months have all but transformed the traditional policy and government of this ancient kingdom.

A few years ago the author had occasion to make a journey to Persia by way of the southern provinces of Russia, following the roads towards the Shah's capital with which Russia's policy of "peaceful penetration" has endowed this portion of the Middle East. From thence, travelling by caravan along the old Bagdad trail

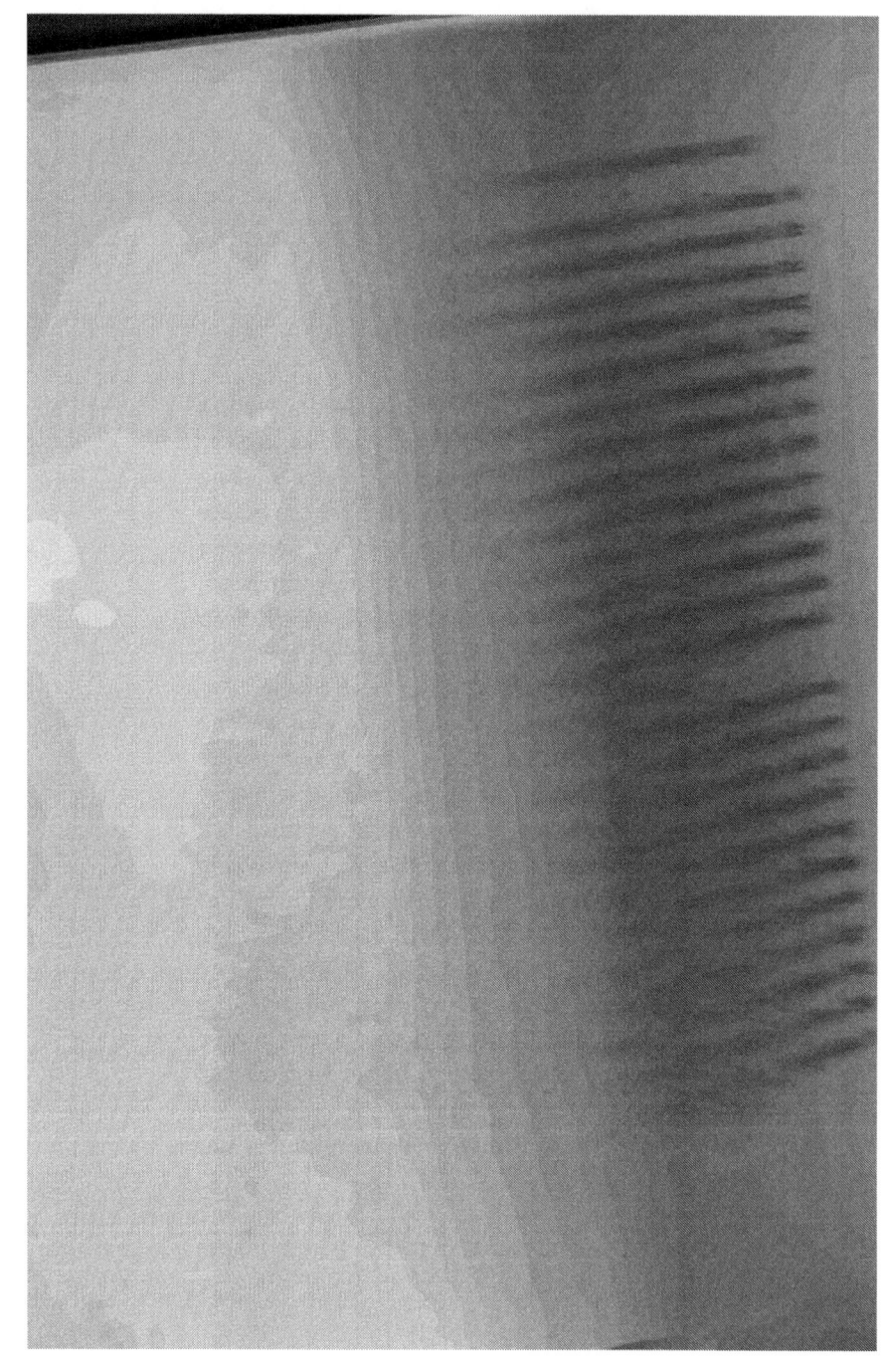

INTRODUCTION

Several of the following chapters have already appeared in the *Illustration* and the *National Geographic Magazine,* and the author's thanks are due the Editors for permission to reproduce them.

PERSIA:

THE AWAKENING EAST

I.

THE THRESHOLD OF ASIA.

THE last stage of our journey across the southern provinces of Russia towards the Shah's dominions lay from Tiflis, the center of Russian rule in the Caucasus, to Baku, the great Petroleum Metropolis on the shores of the Caspian.

Until the recent outbreaks of race hatred and religious fanaticism had somewhat marred their picture of a colonial Utopia, Russian statesmen and journalists were fond of pointing to the wonderful commercial growth of the Caucasus as an example of the benefits of Russian administration among a semi-barbarous people.

As we approached the last outposts of European civilization, and drew near the vague boundary that separates the Empire of the White Czar from his Asiatic neighbors, we were more and more impressed at every step by the strange contrast between the misery and degradation we had

observed on all sides in the older provinces of
Holy Russia and the apparent prosperity of
these picturesque towns and cities of the Caucasian frontier.

Fostered by the generous colonial policy of
M. de Witte—a policy that dotted the far Russian border with modern cities like Dalny and
Krasnovodsk, built in a night to give substance
to the dream of Russian Imperialism, while it left
the moujik of Central Russia to starve on his
barren fields—we found the ancient towns of
the Caucasus fast losing their Oriental traits
and taking on the outward aspect, at least, of
European cities. The Golovinsky Prospect,
that strange street of Tiflis, which has its beginning among the theatres, clubs and palaces of
the European quarter, and ends in the Asiatic
filth and squalor of the Tatar town, was crowded
with handsome equipages and gay with Russian
uniforms and the bright dresses worn by the
women-folk of Georgian and Armenian merchants. In the cafés of the Place de l'Europe
we met moon-faced Tatar merchants and
Georgian chieftains in their picturesque national
costumes, who talked intelligently about the price

of Standard Oil and the American Tariff question; while at the Officers' Club we saw Circassian princes (every one in the Caucasus who lives in a brick house lays claim to that title), dancing graceful Polish dances with the wives and daughters of Russian bureaucrats.

Among the motley throng of domineering officials and subservient Asiatics who filled the broad avenues of Tiflis, the native Caucasians, with their handsome physique and regular features, presented a marked contrast to the stolid Tartar-faced troopers of the conquering race. The Georgian national dress is one of the most graceful and warlike costumes in the world; clad in the flowing " tcherkeska," an arsenal of shining weapons belted about his narrow waist and wearing a tall cap of shaggy sheepskin, the native of Tiflis is a fierce and imposing figure. In private life he may be nothing more warlike than a bazar merchant or a prosperous tailor of the Golovinsky, but as he swaggers about the streets of his native town, toying with the silver hilt of his long Caucasian dagger, one realizes that the Georgian national spirit, after withstanding for centuries the onslaught of all the

great conquerors of Asia, from Tamerlane to
Aga Mohammed, has not yet succumbed to the
despotism of a hundred years of Russian rule.

While the newspapers of St. Petersburg
were talking complacently of Russia's "Mani-
fest Destiny in Asia," and comparing the prosperous condition of the Caucasus with the
famine-stricken provinces of India, the first
mutterings of the approaching storm were beginning to be heard. During our visit the police
were already preparing for the sudden outburst
of barbarism long repressed that a few months
later filled the Caucasus with familiar scenes of
rapine and bloodshed.

As the Trans-Caspian Express, which was
to carry us to Baku, moved out from the new
railway station in Tiflis, we observed that the
broad platforms between the triple line of military sidings were crowded with soldiers wearing
the uniform of every branch of the Russian
service:—Cossacks in gray and silver; dragoons
in sombre green; infantry of the line in dingy
white caps and blouses; smart guardsmen from
St. Petersburg and workmanlike riflemen from
the Trans-Caspian,—waiting transportation to

18

TIFLIS

one point or another of the chain of patrols and garrisons established along the whole length of the railroad, and in every town and hamlet of the Caucasus. This display of armed force was the only visible sign of the fierce internal struggle against Russification that was going on all over the Caucasus—the real key-note of Russia's policy along her Turkish and Persian frontiers; the foundation for the unconvincing prosperity which astonishes the traveller towards the Shah's dominions, as he pauses on the threshold of the Eternal East to take a farewell glimpse of the blessings of European civilization.

Under ordinary conditions, the traveller approaching Persia from the north, following the easy line of access afforded by the Russian railways in the Caucasus, will find the choice of two principal routes open to him. The first of these lies overland through the passes near Mount Ararat, following the general direction of the world-old caravan trail that leads from Tiflis to Tabriz—"the ancient city of Tauris"—still the commercial metropolis of Northern Persia. The lines of the Russian railroad already reach as far as the Persian frontier, where they are met

by the camels and pack-animals of the caravan
trail. It is the declared intention of the Russian
railway officials to prolong this line to Tabriz,
and thence to Teheran, and some preliminary
work has already been done with this end in view.
But at the time of our visit the railroad did not
extend beyond the little Persian town of Julfa,
and rather than trust ourselves to the mercies of
the Persian post-service we decided to take the
alternate route to Teheran, which lies partly by
sea from Baku across the treacherous fog-bound
waters of the Caspian to Enzeli, the principal
port of Northern Persia. From this place an
excellent post-road, built by a Russian company,
leads directly to the capital.

For some time after leaving Tiflis our train
wound its way through the deep valleys and
gorges that surround the town. The views of
the " Frosty Caucasus " seen from the car window rival any similar spectacle to be seen in
Switzerland. The granite hill-sides clothed with
forests of shadowy pine trees slope steeply upward to where snow-covered peaks tower to meet
the deep blue of the southern sky. Mountain
torrents roar along by the side of the railway,

which for long distances is hewn from the solid
rock of the mountain's flank. One rarely sees
other signs of habitation than the ruins belonging to a stormy past—the crumbling brick towers
of Persian and Georgian castles that still challenge each other across the valleys, or now and
again, the empty round-arch windows of some
deserted Byzantine monastery. At rare intervals we passed neat villages clustering about the
new white dome of a Russian church, or an
isolated farm-house with strong walls and narrow windows, loop-holed for defense.

Nightfall found us leaving the mountains
and entering upon broad plains or steppes, covered with coarse yellow grass. Here the few
stations where our train halted were apparently
set down arbitrarily in an empty waste. Near
each of these buildings stood a tall framework
of wood, from the summit of which a brown-
coated sentinel kept a lookout over the plain.

Bare and unattractive as these steppes appear, as we approached the shores of the Caspian,
early next morning, the scene became even more
wild and desolate. Here, nearly all signs of
vegetation disappear, while on every side the

surface of the plain is broken by low volcanic hills and ridges wrought into fantastic shapes by wind and rain. Great sloughs of mud and pools of oily water give to the landscape an unsubstantial appearance, as though the earth's crust were still in process of formation. This in a measure is actually the case, and the scenery of the greater part of the peninsula of Bala-Khané might be said to belong to some earlier epoch of the world's existence.

Yet in spite of its barren and unattractive appearance, the province of Baku is one of the richest in the Czar's empire. As we drew near the city of Baku we could see on every side the gaunt wooden scaffoldings marking the sites of countless oil-wells rising from the treeless plain. On sidings near the railway stood long rows of tank-cars filled with crude petroleum awaiting transportation across the Isthmus; and lines of oil-pipe, writhed like great serpents among the hills, conveying the naphtha from the oil-fields to the refineries near Baku. The horizon was darkened by a dense pall of smoke that hangs perpetually over the suburb known as Tchorne-Gorod—" the Black Town "—where the largest of these establishments are situated; while every breeze that came through the car windows was heavy with the familiar reek of coal-oil.

At the time of our visit to Baku the whole population appeared animated by the spirit of feverish enterprise and boundless optimism that characterizes the citizens of a mining camp in the West of America while enjoying the pleasing influences of a " boom." And to the picturesque features of frontier life in Nome or Goldfield was added the strange contrasting spectacle of an ancient Oriental city in transformation. Since its foundation, in the dim ages of the past, Baku has been the spoil of every new race of conquerors who in their turn have made themselves masters of the shores of the Caspian. Each succeeding horde has left its mark on the local architecture and population, so that Baku stands to-day a bewildering mosaic made up from Persian, Turkish, Georgian, and Russian elements. Clustering about the base of a steep hillside rise the houses of the Asiatic town, tier on tier of crumbling walls and wooden lattice-work; the bright golden cupolas of a Russian cathedral and a large new barrack occupying the summit of this eminence—by far the most conspicuous buildings in the town.

In the Russian quarter, tall buildings of modern construction are everywhere taking the place of the Tatar habitations. Side by side with the winding alleys and tortuous streets of the old Bazar, one finds boulevards lined with handsome modern shops and the new residences of government officials. Even in the Persian town signs of European progress are visible on every hand. An American trolley line winds its way among the crumbling hovels of the Oriental suburb, and at night the white glare of arc lights falls strangely on the tiled domes and minarets of Mohammedan mosques and baths.

From the railway station we were driven to our lodgings in a neat vehicle with rubber-tired wheels, but in place of the bearded moujik of St. Petersburg or Odessa, the driver's seat was occupied by a tall Georgian wearing a sheepskin kolpak, and with a knife at least two feet long hanging from a leathern girdle about his waist. A half-broken team of Tatar ponies, hitched three abreast, carried us at a great rate of speed

over deep ruts and piles of frozen mud that encumbered the broad unpaved streets, while our
driver occasionally glanced back at us with a triumphant grin as we raced past other " drosh-
kies " or scattered a crowd of Asiatics at some
busy street-corner. Our wild ride ended before
the principal hotel, which occupied the palace of
some departed Persian vizir, a massive structure
with vaulted arcades built around three sides of
a dingy interior court-yard. Our apartments
were entered through an opening that served at
the same time as door and window. A wash-
stand and a rickety camp-bed covered with a thin
layer of dingy linen was the only furniture at
our disposal, and on attempting to wash away
the stains of travel we found the water in the
cracked basin covered with a thick greasy scum
of petroleum.

From these unattractive surroundings we
soon descended to the coffee-room of the hotel,
which was filled by a noisy cosmopolitan throng
of " oil men," who sat at rough deal tables, drinking Ruinart and Moet and Chandon from thick
tumblers, with that careless contempt which is
bred only of long familiarity. Champagne is

apparently one of the rare European luxuries to be obtained in unlimited quantities in Baku, and even the shabbiest habitués were drinking it like water. The latter beverage we found but little used, as the springs of the Bala-Khané peninsula are so impregnated with naphtha that the waters are unfit for human consumption. Only the native Tatar population, whose stomachs appear to be equal to the task of assimilating anything short of crude petroleum, drink from them with impunity.

The atmosphere of the low-vaulted room was blue with the smoke of Persian tobacco, and heavy with the stench of oily boots and clothing. Most of our fellow guests were shouting at the top of their voices: a babel of half the languages of Europe and Asia. Many of those present were dressed in clothes of a more or less European pattern; but nevertheless it was easy to recognize the Oriental features of Jews, Armenians, Tatars, and Persians, belonging to the merchant class, who were apparently fast adapting themselves to the polite manners and customs of the dominant race. That evening we made the acquaintance of several English and American

A GEORGIAN OF BAKU

THE OIL FIELDS—BALA-KHANÉ

engineers employed by the foreign companies at the oil-fields, and sat for some time listening to stories of " strikes " and " gushers "—of poor men grown rich in a day, and of great fortunes that literally " went up in smoke " in a few hours. For even at the time when the incendiary's torch and mob violence were unknown in Baku, the haunting fear of a conflagration hung over the Russian oil-fields.

* * * * * * * *

Marco Polo, in his wonderful book of travels, speaks of Bala-Khané as follows:

" On the confines towards Georgianna there is a fountain from which oil springs in great abundance, insomuch that a hundred ship-loads might be taken from it at one time. This oil is not good to use with food, but it is good to burn, and is also used to anoint camels that have the mange. People come from vast distances to fetch it, for in all countries around have they no other oil."

The oil-fields of Bala-Khané were exploited many centuries before the arrival of the Russians, but it is only within the last twenty years that the commerce in naphtha has become the most important industry of the Caucasus. Good Ser Marco would have been surprised to know that future generations would find in his " burning spring " a mine of riches compared to which the treasures of Golconda pale into insignificance, and that on the desert near-by would arise a great city peopled by a restless throng of wealth-seekers drawn from every corner of the globe.

The drive from the railway station to the oil-fields lay along a slippery road, deep with oily mud into which our conveyance sank almost to the hub. By the wayside, half-naked Tatars were busily skimming the waste oil from the surface of slimy pools and rivulets, and our guide told us that even at this miserable business they make an excellent profit. To touch foot to the ground meant irretrievable ruin to boots and clothing, so that every one (even the natives) rode, and a file of rickety vehicles stretched in a continuous procession along the narrow highway. Every form of wheeled conveyance was represented, from spring wagons of American make to high Turcoman carts set on enormous wheels often eight feet or more in diameter.

The surface of the country surrounding the oil-fields seemed literally to exude crude petroleum, and the stench from the slough through which we were slowly travelling was indescribable, although fortunately by this time we were beginning to grow accustomed to the odor.

As we approached nearer the clank of pulleys and windlass filled the air. In every one of the tall timber pyramids that covered the mouth of the narrow "borings" a Tatar workman watched the simple mechanism that lets down a long metal bucket into the bowels of the earth and draws it up filled with crude petroleum mixed with water and sand. Within recent years American tools and methods have increased the output of the wells a hundred fold. The present system of boring is copied from the methods used in the Pennsylvania oil-fields, and many of the engineers who direct the operation for the Russian companies are Americans or Englishmen. In the old days under the reign of the petroleum monopoly, the Russian *concessionaires* were content to confine their operations to enlarging the natural wells and springs of naphtha which rise to the surface of the earth all over the plateau of Bala-Khané. But with the advent of foreigners these primitive methods have been abandoned. The wells are now sunk far down through sand and rock in search of rich strata and fresh beds of oil-sand, and the costly instruments used represent the triumph of years of Yankee ingenuity and experience in the oil-fields of the New World. In spite of fears to the contrary, there appears no end to the supply of crude petroleum. Even at the time of their maximum output, the flow of oil from the wells of Baku was apparently undiminished. Under the plateau of Bala-Khané lies an underground sea of naphtha, and in some places but a few yards of oil-soaked earth covers this natural reservoir. Once the " crust " has been pierced by the drill, the oil comes gushing of its own accord to the surface, driven by the force of natural gases. Just before the riots of 1905, the yearly output of the oil-wells of Baku amounted to more than twelve and one-half million tons of refined oil, and the most important problem confronting the oil companies was that of mutually limiting their output in order to keep the price at a profitable figure.

During our visit to Bala-Khané we had an opportunity to view at close quarters the wild hordes of Tatar workmen employed in the oil-fields. A more abject and degraded lot of human beings it would be difficult to find anywhere on the face of the earth. Their villages of mud huts were set down on the treeless, sandy plain, far enough away from the wells for them to light their cooking fires in safety, and here we found the stench of oil, added to the all-pervading odors of Oriental housekeeping, almost overpowering. Some of the foreign companies make a pretense of housing their workmen in long wooden sheds, which are forcibly cleaned at rare intervals, but by far the greater number live in rough encampments, where they are at liberty to satisfy their own ideals of comfort and sanitation.

Most of these workmen in the oil-fields are Mohammedans, and strange to say their piety is a source of constant annoyance to their employers. In view of the recent controversy in the American newspapers concerning the oil "tainted" contributions of a well-known magnate to the funds of a foreign missionary society, the following incident of our visit to the oil-fields of Bala-Khané may not be without interest. As we were being shown through the pumping-house belonging to a Russian company, our guide, a sturdy Dutchman from the oil-fields of Pennsylvania, suddenly came upon a Tatar workman, lying prostrate, his face toward Mecca, on a strip of greasy carpet among the idle machinery. Without giving him time to struggle to his feet, our friend raised him more suddenly than gently with a well-applied kick:

"Choist look at dese fellows!" he exclaimed, indignantly; "ve haf to vatch dem or dey pray de whole tam time!"

"Vat mit Mohammedan feast days and Russian saints' days ve get no vork done at all. Vat ve need is a cargo of good missionaries to convert de whole tam lot!" he added, vindictively.

Here is a new aspect of the missionary question, which has, perhaps, never been given proper consideration at home!

Shortly after the commencement of the Japanese war, a general strike broke out at Baku, and the wild workmen of Bala-Khané marched on the town, leaving behind them, in place of the scene of busy industry I have described, the fire-blackened ruins of a few pump-houses and the burning craters of hundreds of oil-wells. Thus, in the short space of a few hours the petroleum industry of Baku was literally wiped from the face of the earth. But while the oil-fields have never recovered their former productiveness, the damage is now being gradually repaired, and Russian oil once more supplies the markets of Southern Europe and the Middle East.

II.

ACROSS THE CASPIAN.

THE little Russian steamer that plies across
the Caspian from Baku to Enzeli lay awaiting
our arrival at the end of a long wooden pier
stretching for several hundred yards across the
shallow, oily waters of the Bay of Baku. Although every available inch of space on her lower
deck was long since occupied by merchandise
or passengers, a crowd of late comers still bat-
tled about the narrow gangway, those in the rear
pushing blindly forward in their anxiety not to
be left behind, while the front rank howled in
dismal chorus under the rough handling of half
a dozen stalwart Cossack policemen.

The lot of the poor creatures who travelled
third class along with a full deck-load of merchandise, was anything but an enviable one.
Penned together more like animals than human
beings, with scarcely room to lie down on the
filthy decks, they were forced to remain almost
without moving until the end of the voyage was
reached. The wiser ones, covering themselves

with their rugs and blankets, with the help of a heavy dose of opium soon forgot their troubles in sleep, while those who could not afford this luxury passed their time as best they might, smoking, scratching, and squabbling sociably with their neighbors.

Seen from an upper deck, reserved for the wealthier class of native passengers and for European travellers, the forward part of our little steamer presented a curious spectacle. Among our motley crowd of fellow-passengers were to be found strange types and costumes from every quarter of the Middle East; wild Georgian and Circassian tribesmen in tall *kol-paks* of sheepskin; grave Bokhariot merchants in snowy turbans; moon-faced Tatars from Trans-Caspia, with little embroidered skull-caps set jauntily on their shaven skulls; Armenians in their sombre national costume, their broad belts heavy with silver ornaments; Kurdish peasants, workmen from the oil-fields of Bala-Khané in helmet-like caps of brown felt; and Persian merchants from the bazars of Resht and Teheran in tall astrakhan caps and flowing robes of brown or dove-color;—men of every race and creed sitting knee to knee, shoulder to shoulder, their differences for the moment set aside.

We shared the Captain's cabin with a party of Persian officials homeward bound after a visit to the capitals of Europe. These, unlike their picturesque fellow-countrymen, were dressed according to their ideas of European fashion. One tall gentleman who told me that he was "a Court Poet of Teheran" favored me with a great deal of his company throughout the voyage. This follower of Saadi and Háfiz had even abandoned the picturesque "kaftan" or cap, worn by all Persians of the official class, and appeared in a round-topped "bowler" or Derby, while the rest of his costume to Western eyes appeared equally unpoetical: a light blue necktie decorated with painted flowers, light trousers with a broad check, and a fancy waistcoat— scarcely the apparel one would expect to find worn by a disciple and fellow-countryman of Omar Khayyám!

He appeared to be leaving Europe with considerable reluctance, and expressed a fear that I should find the capital of Persia somewhat *triste* after the life of Paris and

ON THE OLD CARAVAN ROAD, NEAR RESHT

London. A laudable desire to exercise a slight knowledge of French kept the "mirza" (the modern Persian equivalent of "scribe") at my side for hours at a time. Even when I retired to my stuffy cabin he still pursued me with gentle insistance, but fortunately not far from Baku a light ground swell commenced to ruffle the calm surface of the Caspian, and to my intense relief my Oriental friend subsided into an unsociable heap near the smokestack, while his deep groans and prayers to Allah—in the purest vernacular—were heard all over the ship.

The morning of the second day after leaving Baku found us lost in the mazes of a black Caspian fog, somewhere in the neighborhood of Enzeli, our port of destination. Our position was not without danger, for at frequent intervals an ominous bump, followed by a long wail from the frightened passengers forward, reminded us of the near vicinity of the dangerous bar that blocks the mouth of the most important seaport of Northern Persia.

For several hours we lay almost motionless, surrounded by a gray wall of impenetrable mist, when in answer to the ceaseless blowing of our whistle a long surf-boat manned by eight wild-looking natives of the Caspian marshes came off to meet us from the shore. The rowers spoke a mongrel Turkish dialect, which even our polyglot captain was unable to understand; but, after a long parley it appeared that the small launch, which is used to convey passengers across the bar, had been abroad looking for us since daybreak. After a couple of hours more of dreary waiting she at last appeared, and transferring our luggage to her narrow deck we started towards the invisible land.

Presently through the rising mists we caught sight of Enzeli, a large village of squalid huts standing near the water's edge. The miserable fever-stricken inhabitants came running down to the landing-place to greet us, begging for coppers and quinine, a drug which appears to be considered a great luxury in this malarious locality! After our effects had been listlessly examined by a fever-stricken Belgian official, one of those in charge of the customs administration since the floating of the last Russian loan, we were free to embark once more and continue our journey across a broad lagoon to

Pireh-Bazar, a suburb of the ancient Persian town of Resht.

Our arrival at Pireh-Bazar was the signal for a rush to the landing stage of a crowd of shouting porters and camel-drivers, and in less time than it takes to tell, we found ourselves borne bodily to the shelter of a mud caravansary, where a group of Persian merchants were drinking tea about a battered samovar. A handful of copper coins having stilled the popular demand for " backshish," we were allowed to thaw our stiffened limbs before the tiny fire, while a carriage was prepared to carry us over the several miles of rough road that separates Pireh-Bazar from Resht.

The contrast between the orderly spectacle of the busy docks of Baku and the disorder and confusion which reigns at Enzeli and Pireh-Bazar, was very striking. The manner of handling the considerable volume of trade that passes through the principal port of Northern Persia has probably remained unchanged for the last thousand years. We found the muddy banks of the canal for some distance above and below the caravansary littered with every con-

ceivable variety of merchandise, piled at random
without protection from the weather, awaiting
the arrival of the caravans from the interior.
Many boxes and bales bore the trade-marks of
European firms, and to judge from their appearance had been lying there for some time. A
great number of the boxes from Europe were
flimsy wooden affairs, quite unfitted to stand
the rough usage of caravan travel, or else of
such a size that even an elephant would have
found difficulty in carrying them. On account
of this ignorance on the part of foreign merchants of the conditions in Persia, much of the
merchandise sent from Europe is taken from the
original package and roughly packed at Pireh-
Bazar by the camel-drivers; nor is it astonishing, under these conditions, that a large part of
their contents is spoiled or pilfered during the
operation.

We had been warned by the accounts of
previous travellers of the fallen estate of the
ancient capital of the province of Mazanderan,
yet I must confess to being somewhat disappointed by my first view of a large Persian city.
We approached Resht through a wide suburb of

ruined houses and gardens, and found ourselves at last in a long, narrow street lined by high mud walls which effectually shut out all view of the premises within. This we afterwards found was the most fashionable quarter of the town, and behind these unattractive barriers were hidden gardens and handsome villas belonging to the rich merchants and officials of the place. As we approached nearer the center of the town we came to a more populous street, where from every doorway bands of frowzy children, rushed out to shout and stare at us as we passed, while troops of mangy dogs, the street-cleaning department of Resht, arose reluctantly from their all-day siestas in the middle of the road and added their protesting voices to the general outcry.

Often the way was so narrow that the pedestrians we met were obliged to seek refuge in neighboring doorways, or to flatten themselves against the mud walls to allow us to pass. Once on rounding a corner we came unexpectedly on a group of camels resting on the shady side of a little market-place, and their sudden appearance so frightened our team of gaunt Persian steeds that we were all but thrown out into the black filth of the roadway.

The residence of the Governor of Mazanderan, an ornate building covered with execrable stucco work in the modern Persian style, a couple of half-ruined mosques with crumbling minarets, and a huge empty bazar which I visited later in the day on a vain quest for rugs and curios, were apparently the only public buildings worthy of notice. Altogether the attractions of Resht hardly seemed to warrant a prolonged stay, and we determined to push on with all possible speed towards Teheran.

At this point, however, a new difficulty presented itself. Our host of the so-called " European Hotel," where we were spending the night, in answer to our inquiries concerning a post-carriage to convey us further on our journey, informed us that on account of some official function in progress at the Capital, the only available conveyances on the new Russian road had all been engaged for days ahead. Declining the miserable service of " chapar " ponies, which are ridden from post to post, we had almost made up our minds to continue our journey on horseback in the old-fashioned way, when a resourceful Armenian appeared on the scene, who declared himself ready to transport us to Teheran—offering us the use of a small carriage drawn by a couple of sorry Persian ponies. This arrangement obliged us to leave a large part of our luggage behind, but any alternative seemed preferable to spending a week or perhaps longer in wandering about the filthy streets of Resht, so " Harnessing the Chariot of Opportunity with the Horses of Necessity," as our Persian friends would say, we closed the bargain for a sum that seemed ridiculously small, although in reality about twice as much as the tariff of the post-road allowed.

Early the next morning the dingy " saki " of the establishment awoke us at daybreak, and we set off on our five days' journey, amid the blessings of a crowd of beggars, obligingly present to enable us to secure good fortune for our journey by contributing to their wants. After an adventurous drive through the crowded bazars, we at last left behind us the deep ruts and pitfalls of the streets of Resht and rolled smoothly out over the hard surface of the new

Russian post-road. In front of a neat stone building painted with the official black and white stripes familiar to all who have travelled in the Czar's empire, we paused to pay toll as far as Teheran. Here a Russian official wearing a smart blue uniform provided us with a paper in Russian and Persian, giving us access to all the post-houses along the route. At the same time a ragged Persian sentinel armed with an old musket attempted to levy tribute on his own account, commencing in bold official tones and descending the scale of persuasion until finally he ended in a whining appeal for a few shahis to keep him from starvation.

The road leading from the shores of the Caspian to the capital of Persia has been open to general traffic for several years. Considered merely as a financial investment, the million and a half dollars expended in building this fine highway may seem out of all proportion to the returns, but there can be no question as to the important part it has played in forwarding Russian interests in Northern Persia. Its fame has gone abroad through every caravansary of the Middle East, and where a railroad would have

TRAVELLING MERCHANTS

HUNGRY PEASANTS—MAZANDERAN

disturbed a host of ancient customs and privileges dear to the inhabitants of the country, this new way has only lightened the difficulties and hardships that once beset travellers and traffic on the old caravan road.   New villages are springing up everywhere along the route, and the Russians take good care that the inhabitants should know that to Russian enterprise alone this happy change in their fortunes is due.

The engineering work of the Resht post-road has been carried out in a thoroughly durable manner.   Often hewn from the solid rock of the mountain-side, or crossing deep ravines by girder bridges of the most modern construction, it forms a striking example of the Russian policy of " peaceful penetration " that owes its inception to the real " strong man " of Russia, Serge de Witte.

Following the natural path of least resistance, sometimes high above us on the mountain-side, sometimes winding along the valley below, I could make out the fading gray streak of what was once the old Persian caravan track.   From time immemorial this ancient road had been the great commercial highway between the shores of

the Black Sea and the rich provinces of Northern
Persia. Most of the trade of Khorassan still
follows this route until it reaches the Russian
railways in the Caucasus, while merchandise
transported from Russia is sold in every bazar,
as far as the Afghan frontier.

The post-carriages and four-wheeled freight-
wagons brought from Europe are still comparatively rare, and the greater part of the merchandise is carried by means of caravans and
droves of pack-animals. During our first day's
journey we passed thousands of camels travelling
in long files stretching sometimes for a quarter
of a mile without a break, each fastened by a
long cord attached to a ring fixed in its super-
cilious nose, to the saddle of the one ahead. The
Bactrian camels used on these cold mountain
trails of Northern Persia are very different in
appearance from the gaunt, apocalyptic beasts
seen in the deserts of Egypt. Indeed, the true
Bactrian is a very handsome animal (judged at
least by the standards of camel beauty), his neck
and shoulders covered with a long growth of soft
brown hair, which hides the rude outlines of his
powerful frame. A good Persian camel is

capable of carrying with ease a load of a thousand pounds, and as they are often the whole fortune of their owners, they are treated with the best of care and attention.

The lighter traffic of the road is carried by horses or mules, the front ranks stepping out bravely enough behind the gayly tasselled bell-mare, while the hinder ranks, the lame and the halt, are beaten along by their relentless " charvadars." Often our carriage was forced to jostle its way through droves of little donkeys huddling together like sheep in the middle of the road, each tiny creature almost hidden beneath its burden of hay or dried brushwood.

Every mile we travelled brought some new scene of Oriental life to vary the monotony of our journey. Sometimes it was a Persian gentleman accompanied by servants and retainers on horseback, followed by a long train of pack-animals carrying his possessions—and wives, the latter slung two by two in " kajavas," rough native " panniers," on either side of a mule or camel. Again a galloping post-carriage drawn by four lean horses or mules would lumber by in a cloud of dust, filled to the roof with Persian travellers, on whom this mode of travel has much the same effect as the first ride in a racing automobile has on an European. Occasionally we would meet a band of wandering darvishs on a begging pilgrimage from village to village; armed with great axes, or other weapons of the heroic days of Islam, their wild locks dyed scarlet with henna juice, and leopard-skins thrown across their shoulders. Or again it was a company of merchants riding together for protection against the dangers of the way, followed by a string of sleek mules laden with the carpet khorjeens that held their wares.

And sometimes we would overtake a troop of ragged Persian infantry on the march, many of the more fortunate riding diminutive donkeys, which they drummed along with their naked heels; or a patrol of Cossacks in the pay of the Russian Company would swagger by, with flashing cartridge-cases and jingling weapons, conscious that the peace of the road is safe in their hands.

The first night of our journey was spent in one of the new Russian " Mimam-Khané " or rest houses. These are neat stone structures, two stories high, built at convenient stopping-places all the way from Resht to Teheran. The first floor is freely open for the accommodation of poorer travellers, while the rooms of the second story, more luxuriously appointed, are hired for a small sum. On the walls of each room hangs a notice in French, Russian, and Persian, giving a list of the articles it contains and the price of each one of them. This serves to discourage the frugal habits of Persian travellers, who might otherwise burn up the (to them) superfluous chairs and tables as firewood.

In most of these post-houses the traveller is expected to furnish his own food, but as we wished to keep our supply of canned provisions for possible emergencies, we made our first meal off a couple of the innkeeper's tough Persian fowls, which were brought in with much ceremony on top of a huge mound of rice. With our appetites sharpened by our long ride in the keen air, we ate heartily, and what was left fell to the lot of our coachman and his assistants.

Almost all Persians seem to possess the knack of cooking rice, and everywhere throughout Persia we found it excellent. Chickens are to be had in almost any village and these birds, cooked in every possible style, form the constant diet of the Persian traveller. On rare occasions mutton can be obtained, but as beef and pork are considered "unclean" by all good Mussulmans even the neediest Persian will scorn to prepare or even touch them. For this reason, unless wild game is to be had, the Persian bill of fare is somewhat limited, and it is advisable to carry a sufficient supply of prepared food when undertaking a journey of any length.

Let me further add for the benefit of future travellers, that unless they are prepared for disagreeable surprises, it is best that they should refrain from inquiring too closely into the mysteries of Persian culinary methods. Only once did I attempt to confirm my suspicions on this point, and the experience taught me that as long as I might be at the mercy of Persian cooks, it would be "folly to be wise." Indeed, I know of one case, that of a Minister Plenipotentiary, who after weeks of wrestling with time-honored customs, resigned himself at last to a diet of such dishes as he could prepare over a spirit lamp.

All night the camel-bells of passing caravans clanged beneath our window, effectually banishing sleep, and the next morning found us early astir and impatient to be off. Our second day's journey lay through a marshy country, like that about Resht, constantly overhung by the damp sea mists that rise from the Caspian. Here the vegetation grows in rank profusion, and one sees on every side broad fields of pale green rice-plants, which form the principal crop of the province of Mazanderan. The continual dampness rots the limbs and branches from the trees, leaving only the swollen trunks covered with moss and parasitic vines which present a very curious appearance. The inhabitants of the country are all pitiful-looking creatures, racked by the agues and fevers of the marshy soil, quite unlike the sturdy peasants who have been our fellow passengers on the steamboat.

The road, however, rises constantly, and towards evening we were passing through a fertile country covered with forests of oak and hemlock, where broad meadows gave pasture to flocks of sheep and herds of camels and asses. Small gray cattle, with humps on their shoulders

51

like the " sacred " cows of India, were also quite
numerous.   These, however, are only kept for
their milk, on account of the prejudice every
Persian has against eating beef.   Nestling
among the shady groves were prosperous villages and occasionally we came upon the country
house of some wealthy landowner, set in broad
gardens, the whole surrounded by high mud
walls.

Nightfall found us among the foothills of
the El Bruz range, their upper levels already
glittering white with new-fallen snow.   The
caravans we met were all hurrying along to escape the threatened fall, as in winter the mountain roads are often blocked for weeks at a time.
Our driver and his brazen-lunged assistant sent
our ill-matched team along at a very fair rate of
speed, profiting by every descent of the road to
urge them into a mad gallop which only ceased
when the upward ascent forced them to stop from
sheer exhaustion.   There was a spice of danger
and excitement about these wild dashes through
the keen mountain air, for on one side of the
road the vertical face of the mountain-side towered above us, while on the other came the sheer

fall of a precipice, with the faint sound of a mountain stream brawling over the stones far below. Fortunately, by some miracle, the crazy harness held together, and as our only upset was towards the inner side of the road, we escaped without serious injury. When we reached the higher altitudes the horses began to suffer cruelly from the rarefied air, and we were forced to make frequent stops to allow them to rest. The driver would then resort to a peculiar system of "massage," vigorously rubbing the heads and shoulders of the panting beasts with his bare hands, ending with a strong downward pull on either ear. It is doubtful whether this latter process affords much real relief, but we found it a generally accepted theory throughout Persia.

As we entered the mountains the cliffs on both sides of the valley presented a very curious appearance on account of the quantities of copper and other minerals they contain. Some are of light yellow or pink, while others of a deep red color gave the effect of being in a molten condition, which contrasted strangely with the patches of white snow at their feet.

This sinister region is also interesting on

account of the legends that connect it with the bloody doings of the strange sect known in history as the "Assassins." Here the followers of Saba Hassan, the terrible "Old Man of the Mountains," had their stronghold, and exercised their cruelties on the unfortunate travellers who passed along the old caravan trail. Near the present road a castle is still pointed out as the headquarters of these worthies, whose very name has become synonymous with murder and cowardly crime.

On the morning of the fourth day of our journey, the steep road we had been following into the mountain gave a final lift through a rocky pass; then, instead of descending once more, we found ourselves on the edge of a rolling plain, stretching away from the foot of the mountains at our back, as far as the eye could reach. Seen from the level of the plateau the chain of the El Bruz, which towers so grandly over the lowlands of the Caspian, becomes little more than a range of high hills with here and there some giant peak, like Mount Demavend, rising from amongst them. In contrast with the luxuriant vegetation of the province of Mazan-

deran, the scenery of these Persian highlands
is indescribably barren and desolate. For hours
at a time we travelled across an empty brown
plain, stretching away on every side to a horizon
of low volcanic hills, without a tree or sign of
living green. The straight line of the post-road
marked by the poles of the Indo-European Telegraph, lead us on and on across a desert, silent,
parched, and motionless, except for the dust-
storms that played across its face. Now and
again the white gleam of a salt marsh, seen on
the horizon, or the pearly mist of a distant mirage
would persuade us that we were approaching the
life-giving presence of water, an illusion which
receded or disappeared on our nearer approach.

The traveller, read in the poetry and literature of the Golden East, soon learns to appreciate the Oriental's point of view in judging the
beauties of nature. Compared to the verdant
scenery of Europe, there is little to admire in
the landscape of Northern Persia; yet these
lonely wastes are not without a certain wild
beauty of their own. The great drama of morning and evening tints the desert with wonderful
hues that shift and blend like the changing colors

of the sea, and in the fierce light of noon-day strange cloud shadows play across its surface, relieving the monotonous uniformity of rock and sand.

Contrast, indeed, is the keynote of desert life. No gardens have ever seemed to me half so beautiful as some walled enclosure, filled with scanty rows of orange- and lemon-trees, found at the end of a long day's ride across the arid Persian plain. No fruit has ever had so rare a taste as the little yellow citrons brought us by Persian peasants, in some dusty caravansary, as we lay resting our weary limbs among our saddle bags on the hard mud floor.

To the poets of Persia we owe the common impression that their beloved country is a Land of Gardens and Flowers. Their Oriental imagination has woven a veil of romance about the "fields of Iran," while throughout the greater part of the Shah's dominions the very reverse of this Legend of Fertility is nearer the truth. The life of the Persian peasant is one long struggle with the adverse forces of nature. Such rare cultivation as we saw depended entirely on artificial irrigation by means of underground channels leading to distant reservoirs among the mountains that generations of toilers have hollowed out with infinite pains, often hundreds of feet below the level of the land. The few villages that we passed were miserable collections of mud huts whose inhabitants earned a precarious existence by trading with the travellers along the caravan road. And surrounding these a few fields of grain and vegetables, little squares of irrigated land that look from a distance like green mantles spread out on the arid plain—

> " The strip of Herbage strown
> That just divides the desert from the sown,
> Where name of slave and Sultan is forgot,
> Peace to Mohammed on his golden Throne."

True, for a few brief weeks in the springtime a miracle is wrought on these barren plains. Under the magic spell of the tempered sun and gentle rain, an ephemeral carpet of grass and wild flowers is spread over the stony waste. Then the caravan grazes wide across the plain, and the land is filled with the sound of running water and the scent of growing herbage. But before the withering blasts of the summer winds, this illusion of luxuriance fades quickly away, and in a few brief weeks the Persian desert takes on its normal appearance. In place of meadows strewn with flowers, the traveller finds the gleaming waste of the salt desert; in place of " the bulbul singing on the bow," the vulture and carrion crow rising heavily from their repast; and as league after league of desolation unfolds itself to his view, he realizes that with the exception of a few favored provinces the Persia of which Saadi, and Háfiz, and Omar " the Tent-maker " sang so eloquently, existed largely in their own gifted imaginations.

III.

TEHERAN lies in the midst of a broad rolling
plain thickly covered with flat stones of a dull
bluish color. From a distance this peculiar formation has the appearance of some magic sea
whose billows, crowned by outcroppings of white
salt, have been frozen into sudden immobility.
Across this dreary expanse the narrow post-road
stretched away to the horizon before us, where
in the far distance the rugged outlines of the El
Bruz range and the grand white cone of Mount
Demavend were outlined against the turquoise
Persian sky. Since daybreak we had been hoping, at every moment, to catch our first glimpse
of the towers and minarets of the Persian capital. From time to time, in answer to repeated
questioning, our sleepy driver would wave his
whip in a comprehensive sweep that took in the
whole sky-line ahead, empty of any sign of
habitation except an occasional distant village or
high-walled garden, and muttering a reassuring

... would relapse once more into
... memorousness.

... we met along the lonely
... peasants taking their produce
... on the mass of tiny donkeys, while
... in the distance would appear
... a Persian husbandman
... the wooden plough, drawn by a lean
... across the ungrateful soil. To-
... towns and villages became more
... Teheran itself, lying in a hollow
... invisible until from the
... we suddenly caught sight of
... the "Ark" or Royal Palace
... high mud wall that sur-
... Passing through a gateway
... the work, where an
... waved their brown rags and
... arms, we found ourselves
... from the quiet monotony
... to the crowded, bustling
... Persian town.

... traveller visiting Teheran
... who expects to find in the Shah's
... famous city of the "Arabian

TEHERAN—THE ROYAL PALACE

"*Tahran anja*" would relapse once more into a state of blissful unconsciousness.

The only natives we met along the lonely road were a few peasants taking their produce to market on the backs of tiny donkeys, while now and again in the distance would appear the patriarchal figure of a Persian husbandman driving his rude wooden plough, drawn by a lean ox or a camel, across the ungrateful soil. Towards mid-day houses and villages became more frequent, but Teheran itself, lying in a hollow of the land, remained invisible until from the crest of a low hill we suddenly caught sight of the shining roof of the " Ark " or Royal Palace rising from behind the high mud wall that surrounds the city. Passing through a gateway covered with gayly-colored tile work, where an army of beggars waved their brown rags and shouted an appeal for alms, we found ourselves suddenly transported from the quiet monotony of a desert journey to the crowded, bustling streets of a great Oriental town.

The sentimental traveller visiting Teheran for the first time who expects to find in the Shah's capital some fabulous city of the " Arabian

TEHERAN—THE ROYAL PALACE

Nights " is destined to be disappointed. Persia has long since awakened from her Golden Dream of the Past. Like Japan, the Land of the Lion and the Sun has fallen under the spell of Western ideas, and the Persian of to-day is striving to adapt his ancient civilization to the ways and customs of Europe, with the same energy and lack of discrimination that characterize the victorious sons of Nippon.

In Persian eyes, at least, Teheran is a European city. The wide streets and tree-lined avenues of the newer quarter of the town date from the reign of Shah Nasr-ed-Din, grandfather of the present Shah, who returned from a visit to Europe fired with the ambition of transforming his capital into an Oriental Paris. But the Persian of the lower classes is a fanatical conservative; the strange madness that drives his rulers to leave the blessed shores of Iran to wander in infidel lands beyond the seas, seems to him wholly foreign and distasteful. And, while the result of Nasr-ed-Din's fondness for the things and ways of Europe are to be seen in Teheran on every hand, the large majority of the citizens cling obstinately to the customs of their forefathers, so that the capital of Persia stands to-day a wonderful City of Contrasts, a meeting-place of opposing civilizations, where the old and the new stand side by side in bewildering confusion.

A little more than a century ago Teheran was described by European travellers as a small village in the neighborhood of the ancient city of Rhages or Rei, which was the capital of Persia under the rule of the Arabian Califs. The ruins of this place are still to be seen some six miles from Teheran, but most of its inhabitants moved to the newer city when it became the favorite dwelling-place of the Kajar princes. The Shahs of this dynasty have spent large sums in enlarging and embellishing the city, and while Teheran can scarcely be said to rival the natural beauties of Shiraz or the architectural splendors of Ispahan, it is now considered the metropolis of Persia.

The climate of this part of the Iranian plateau, varying from extreme heat in summer to bitter cold during the winter months, leaves much to be desired. On account of the high elevation, sudden and violent changes of temperature occur; and I remember witnessing, soon after our arrival, the curious spectacle of a rose-garden in full bloom suddenly overwhelmed and buried beneath a fall of early snow. To these discomforts must be added the high winds which raise clouds of choking dust and sand from the broad unpaved streets during the dry months of the year. Nevertheless, Teheran is a very healthy spot, and in spite of the primitive methods of sanitation still in vogue, the death rate among its population remains comparatively low.

The morning after our arrival, accompanied by a " ferrash " (or footman) from the American Legation, we set out to visit the principal sights of the city. The " Street of the Ambassadors," the main thoroughfare of the new quarter of the town, has little to distinguish it from a street in some provincial town of Europe. Comfortable white villas, inhabited by the Court officials, and foreign residents, line it on either side, some standing in high-walled gardens, others built about three sides of an inner court-yard opening toward the street. Little in their architecture is pleasing or remarkable. Only here and there a bright colored band of tile-work or the graceful arch of a gateway reminds the traveller that he is in the heart of the Orient.

Continuing our walk, we passed through a high gate and came to the Tup Maidan, or Artillery Square. The principal ornament of this public place is a curious collection of old cannon, popularly supposed to form part of the defenses of the city. These lie rusting within a rough wooden fence, and are usually carefully guarded by one or two soldiers from the barracks near at hand. While as weapons they may not be very formidable, from the point of view of the antiquarian they quite repay a visit. Some of them are cast in the shape of dragons and other monstrous beasts and date from the reign of Nadir Shah, who brought them here as trophies of his victorious campaign in India, after the sack of Delhi. Others bear the Royal arms of Portugal, and recall the days long past when Persia, one of the foremost military powers of the world, did not fear to measure strength with the greatest nations of Christendom.

One of these antiquated pieces of ordnance has a curious importance in the eyes of all the

THE PEARL CANNON

ON THE BOULEVARD OF DIAMONDS

vagabonds and evil-doers of Teheran. This ancient weapon, known as the "Pearl Cannon," from the fact that a necklace of real pearls once decorated its grim muzzle, possesses the privilege of conferring "bast" or sanctuary, and as long as criminals or debtors remain in its shadow they may claim immunity from pursuit. A miserable group of offenders is usually to be found camped about the steps of the brick platform on which the cannon rests, while officers of the law or relatives of the injured party wait patiently near until hunger shall drive them from the sacred precincts—a scene that offers a strange insight into the processes of Persian judicial procedure.

The "Boulevard of Diamonds," the name of the principal thoroughfare of Teheran, which leads from the Tup Maidan to the great Bazars and the Royal Palace, summons up visions of Oriental magnificence which are far from being realized. This broad, but very dirty highway, one of the new streets which Nasr-ed-Din opened through the labyrinth of the old Asiatic City, we found anything but imposing, although in Persian eyes it no doubt represents the height of civic magnificence. By a strange prejudice,

dear to the Oriental mind, the broad stone side-
walks are given over to itinerant merchants and
their wares, to open-air cafés, and all kinds of
petty industries, while pedestrians mingle with
the carriages and pack-animals that crowd the
middle of the street.

The varied types of humanity that go to
make up the population of the " City of Contrasts " are perhaps never seen to such striking
advantage as on some sunny winter's day on this
favorite promenade of the citizens of Teheran.
Threading his way carefully through the streams
of traffic, a fat mollah ambles by on a lazy mule,
towards the mosque. Next comes a smart
young attaché from the foreign legations on his
way to play polo on the Maidan, or a Cossack
of the Shah's body-guard, dressed as nearly like
a Russian soldier as possible. A Court official
in a Parisian landau, surrounded by a galloping
troop of attendants, goes charging through the
crowd, with loud cries of " Kabardah! Kabardah! " (" Make way! make way! "). Next, a
wild-eyed darvish adds his loud cries to the general confusion, in an insolent demand for the
alms of the Faithful; or a party of Persian

women, in baggy black pantaloons, their faces
hidden by thick linen masks, pass in single file,
under the escort of a negro eunuch. And at
intervals the finishing touch is added to this Oriental scene when a tramway crowded to the roof
with native passengers goes jostling its way
through the long files of camels and pack-horses
on their way to the bazars—perhaps the most
popular European innovation in the Persian
capital.

While the broad streets and squares of the
new quarters of Teheran give the many parts of
the city quite a European appearance, the older
quarters that lie about the bazar still retain all
the characteristics of the Orient. Here, in a
labyrinth of narrow lanes and alleyways, where
even the oldest Teherani often finds himself at a
loss which way to turn, centers the whole commercial life of the city. In Teheran, as in most
of the cities of Northern Persia, the main bazar
consists of a series of long passageways, covered
by a roof of vaulted brick-work. Between the
buttresses that support the roof are narrow
niches which serve as shops and booths, and these
again open at the back into great court-yards or

"caravansaries," where the goods are stored on their arrival, and where the weary camels and pack-animals of the caravan road are stabled after their long journey. Few of the largest of these shops are more than twenty feet square, and the merchant sitting on a narrow ledge or counter before his booth, is within easy reach of every article in his stock, yet the amount of business transacted in this primitive way is often considerable, and many of the bazar merchants are rich men, judged even by the standard of New York and London.

As we passed through the gateway of this vast City of Trade, we found ourselves obliged to move with some caution in the dark interior. The only light filtered in through narrow apertures high in the vaulted roof: bright beams of sunlight that fell in dazzling golden shafts on the passing crowd below. In this maze of shades and shadows our eyes, accustomed to the bright Persian daylight without, could scarcely distinguish what was going on about us. The deafening shouts and cries of buyers and sellers, the thick, choking dust, and the pungent, indescribable " bazar smell," were strangely discon-

A STREET IN TEHERAN

çerting to travellers fresh from scenes of desert
life, and the pure air of the Persian highlands.

All about us the gloom seemed full of sudden dangers. Every few moments we were
obliged to flatten ourselves against the wall to
escape being crushed by the huge bulk of a
passing camel, a file of laden porters, or a drove
of little donkeys charging through the crowd
careless of everything except the cruel goad of
their drivers urging them on. As we advanced,
eager merchants crouching among their wares
reached out clutching at our garments; carpets
were spread in our way; jewelled weapons were
hastily pulled down and thrust upon our attention, while from every side beggars and cripples
pushed and jostled, cursed and implored.

Yet, in spite of all this apparent confusion,
a certain order reigns. Each trade and corpora-
tion has its own quarter where men of the same
calling work side by side. There are streets
where the traveller's ears are deafened by the
pounding of brass and the beating of leather;
more silent ways, hung with bright colors like
those of the cloth-dealers; and others again filled
with pungent smells and spicy odors, where the

perfume-sellers ply their trade. A native seems
always able to discover in what part of this great
Oriental " department store " his needs can be
supplied, but to a foreigner this labyrinth of
strange trades and callings will always remain
something of a mystery.

The traveller who wishes to purchase any
article offered for sale in the bazars of Teheran
soon learns that every commercial transaction in
the Orient must follow an invariable and somewhat irritating mode of progression. The buyer
must first commence with an offer of perhaps
one-fifth of the value of the article he wishes to
purchase, while the seller meets this proposal in
the same spirit, by demanding a price at least
five or six times what it is worth. The struggle
then becomes fast and furious, and all the saints
of the Mohammedan calendar are called upon to
bear witness to the absolute disinterestedness and
candor of the parties concerned. Meanwhile all
the idlers and hangers-on in the neighborhood
gather to take sides, as their inclinations or interest seem to dictate; and to these must be added
all the beggars—the lame, the halt, and the blind
—who are able to get within the circle of spec-

tators, hoping in case a bargain is reached to receive a small share of the amount that changes hands. Thus, it will be seen that even the purchase of such small articles as a Persian water-pipe or a pair of Kurdish saddle-bags becomes an operation of some magnitude in the bazars of Teheran. Tiring at last of these scenes where Oriental cunning played such a transparent rôle, I usually sent a servant to make the purchase of any article that struck my fancy, naming a price that appeared to be the current one; nor was I often disappointed when following this method.

There are still a few good curios to be picked up in the bazars—but a majority of these articles exposed for sale are manufactured in Europe, while most of the native rugs and carpets show the regrettable influence of European patterns and aniline dyes. It is unfortunately true that throughout the East to-day the machine-made products of the unbeliever are everywhere crowding out the fabrics of the old hand-worker. Indeed, many famous Oriental industries are fast disappearing, and the native craftsmen work only for export to the European market, while

71

their compatriots prefer the cheaper if less esthe-
tic patterns of the Occident. Thus, the fine
cloths, once manufactured in Resht and Kashan,
have given way before the products of Manchester and Odessa. Even the coarse canvas-
like stuff, the universal dress of the poorer classes
in Persia, which was once woven during the
winter months on crude native looms, now comes
in greater part from the Yankee mills of Con-
necticut, while New York and Birmingham are
as familiar names to-day in the bazars of
Teheran as were once those of Bokhara and
Bagdad.

A whole quarter of the bazars of Teheran
is given over to the sale of European goods,
usually of the cheapest and shoddiest description.
At one time most of these shops were supplied
with English wares, but of late years the Russians have secured for themselves a lion's share
of the general trade of Northern Persia. Although the Legations of the other powers are all
to be found in a quarter by themselves,—in the
newest part of the town,—the Russian Minister
occupies a house in the native quarter near the
bazars, where he keeps in constant touch with the

center of local activity.   While America and
England, the two greatest commercial powers of
the world, concern themselves but little with
advancing the private interests of their citizens, a
merchant who trades under the flag of the Russian Empire finds in his Consul or Minister a
powerful protector ready to assist him by every
means at his command.   The Russian-Persian
Bank has its branches in every important town
of Northern Persia, where all the advantages of
credit and discount are open to Persian merchants, in their dealings with Russian subjects.
And while the Persian customs were until recently nominally administered by Belgian officials, it is notorious that since the whole financial
situation in Persia passed under the control of
the Russian holders of the last Persian loan,
every revision in the scale of tariffs has been
favorable to Russian trade, often in the face of
bitter protest on the part of the other powers.
Thus, so long as the merchants of other countries
are left by their representatives to shift for themselves in competition with discriminating transport laws, and Russian-built freight roads, there
is little incentive for any but the most adven-

turous trader to enlarge the scope of his business operations in Northern Persia.

Days might be spent by the student of Persian life and character in wandering about the bazars and frequenting the coffee-houses, which abound both within the bazars and in their immediate vicinity. Indeed, " tchai," served in graceful, tulip-shaped glasses, more than half filled with broken lumps of coarse sugar, plays such an important part in the commercial operations of the East, that it is doubtful whether a bargain of any importance could be made without its help.

The whole equipment of even the most fashionable coffee-houses usually consists of little more than an earthen oven and three or four wooden frames, or platforms, made of wood which serve to elevate the patrons of the establishment above the filth of the unswept floor. If the weather permits, these platforms are placed at the door of the establishment, as near as possible to one of the gutters of running water which everywhere intersect the streets of Teheran. A few whiffs from the kalian, which

an attendant " saki " presents in turn to each of
the guests, an occasional sip of sweet tea, and
the sound of water running over the dirty cobbles
in the bottom of some near-by drain, are enough
to keep the average Persian in a state of blissful
" fament " for hours at a time.   When these
pleasures begin to pall, there is always some
neighbor ready for a little desultory bargaining,
or one may listen to the gossip of the " saki," or
the tales and recitations of a professional story-
teller.   As all these luxuries are to be obtained
by the expenditure of the fraction of a penny
for a cup of tea, the *tchai-khané* are one of the
most popular institutions of the Persian bazars.

The professional story-teller is a useful and
always welcome member of society in a country
where only a small proportion of the inhabitants
are able to read and write.   His repertory is
sometimes original, but more often consists of
time-honored tales (many of them known to
Europeans through the translations of Burton),
for to the Oriental mind an old tale, like old
wine, only grows the better with age.

The story-teller, if his stories are well told,
is always sure of a harvest of dingy " shahis,"

but, wise in his generation, he usually pauses to take up his little collection just before the climax of his tale is reached, and should this fall short, he can always extract a few more coins from his auditors with the threat of leaving them in doubt as to the outcome. I recommend this plan to some of our own underpaid scribes who favor the serial form!

It is strange to see about the bazars the many soldiers in uniform who pursue the calling of shop-keepers along with their military duties. As a time-honored custom in Persia makes a large percentage of the pay of the private soldier the recognized perquisite of his superior officers, the rank and file are obliged to depend on other means of income besides their military pay. The prestige of the uniform, however, amply compensates for the drawbacks of military service, and there are countless little ways of turning even so minor an official position as private in the guards to good account. The favorite calling for military men appears to be the not inappropriate trade of butcher. It is a familiar sight to see a military post, guarding some public

RAM FIGHTING—A FAVORITE PERSIAN SPORT

building, decorated with the bloody remains of a freshly-killed sheep, and while the prices may be a little higher than elsewhere, the house-keepers in the vicinity usually find it to their advantage to deal at the " official " shop.

A visit to the Maidan or parade ground of Teheran during a drill is an amusing and in-structive spectacle. On the invitation of a genial Italian who holds the rank of General in the Shah's service, we accompanied him thither one morning to attend a muster of the garrison. The Maidan is a broad, dusty field near the royal palace, entered through a plastered gateway ornamented with the life-size figures of Persian soldiers in modern uniform, painted in bright colors by some native artist.

Except when the foreign colony gather there twice a week to play polo, the Maidan is usually given over to rag-picking, carpet-clean-ing, and other peaceful pursuits, but on the morning of our visit we found it crowded with troopers in motley uniforms representing every branch of the Persian service. Few of the private soldiers could boast of an entire equip-ment, and their " uniforms " were often pieced out with sheepskin "kaftans," baggy Persian trousers, and sheepskin coats, although some of the officers wore uniforms copied after those worn in European countries.

Across the face of the plain moved a wavering line of infantry and cavalry, while a couple of field-guns were drawn about amid much shouting and beating of the straining, raw-boned horses. The general trend of the maneuvers was a little difficult to follow, but doubtless they gave entire satisfaction to the officials from the war office for whose benefit they were carried out:—a couple of exceedingly stout gentlemen in black frock coats, who sat smoking placidly in the shelter of a small tent.

With the exception of a couple of cavalry regiments drilled by Russian officers, the garrison of Teheran is composed of a Falstaffian rabble, more in evidence about the bazars and streets of the capital than in the barracks or on the parade grounds. A few reluctant recruits are sometimes to be found at drill, under the eye of a native officer, who walks up and down the ranks followed by an attendant carrying his sword and water-pipe. But the rank and file are usually too busy earning their living as porters or shop-keepers to be able to pay much attention to such details of military life.

The Persian army has passed through many vicissitudes since the glorious days of the Nadir Shah, and within the last twenty years has probably been " reorganized " oftener than any similar body of troops in the world. During this time the Shah's soldiers have known periods of English, French, and Austrian influence, when officers detailed in turn from each of these powers have done their best to undo the work of their predecessors and to teach the young Persian idea how to shoot according to their own manual and standards.

A few years ago Persia called to her aid instructors from the Czar's army, and at the present day the only troops in Persia efficiently drilled and equipped according to European standards, are the Shah's Cossack " Body Guard," officered by Russians detailed for this service. Many of the privates in this *corps d'elite* are deserters from the Czar's armies in the Caucasus, and should the Russians ever take it into their heads to retrieve their tarnished laurels by marching an army across the frontier along the new road leading from the Caspian to the Persian capital, they will find themselves face to face with troops the exact counterpart of their own in drill and equipment. Just how these regiments will act in the event of such trying circumstances, is a question every one in Teheran is asking, with the possible exception of the Persian military authorities themselves.

The latest rumor from Teheran has it that the Persian army is again to be " reorganized," this time by Japanese officers. It is certain that the victories of the Mikado's forces have been followed with sympathetic interest throughout the whole of the Orient. The spell of European superiority has been broken, and the horrors of the Indian mutiny and of the Russian massacres in Central Asia have long been forgotten. In view of the troubled condition of the Caucasus, and the natural sympathy of the Persians for their fellow Mohammedans under Russian rule, the question of Persian military reform becomes an important one to the peace of the world. There is no dearth of fine material in Persia for an army, and should the young Shah decide

to call to his aid military advisers from the victorious troops of the Mikado, the problem of
the Awakening East will be brought nearer to
Europe than ever.

IV.

NEAR the end of the Boulevard of Diamonds stands the Ark, or Royal Palace, once the citadel of Teheran. Succeeding Shahs of the Kajar dynasty have added to the old fortress and embellished its surroundings, until at the present day several acres of gardens and palaces are contained within a high double-walled enclosure. This latter is a massive barrier of brick-work, unimpressive except for its height and extent, entered at irregular intervals by gateways gay with bright-colored stucco- and tile-work, while over the top of the frowning parapet one catches a glimpse of the shining roofs and minarets of the buildings within, a constant challenge to the curiosity of the traveller.

Naturally it is the ambition of every European who visits Teheran for the first time to penetrate the well-guarded portals of this mysterious domain. This favor, however, does not fall to the lot of every one, and it was only through the courtesy of a high official of the

Court that we were able to visit the interior of
the palace, and to view the somewhat incongruous wonders it contains.

In spite of the theories of modern consti-
tutional monarchy brought back by Nasr-ed-Din
from his trip to Europe; in spite of the " Council ᴸ
of Ministers," " The National Assembly," and
other forms of parliamentary rule, the Royal
Palace has always remained the real nucleus of
the Persian Government. The Shah, until very
lately, still held the life of every one of his
subjects in the hollow of his hand, and about the
person and residence of the sovereign centers all
the interests and subtle influences that guide the
policy of an Oriental state. From behind silken
curtains and carved lattice may come a whisper,
more potent to set the telegraph clicking in a
dozen capitals of Europe than all the rulings of
the grave figure-heads who make up the Shah's
Imperial Council; and the diplomat accredited to
the Court of Teheran soon learns to read the
suave periods of the official reports with an atten-
tive ear open to catch the latest rumor from the
great hive of the " Ark," where some thousand

of courtiers and official "hangers-on," to say
nothing of their wives and families, are gathered
about the person of the sovereign like bees about
a honey-pot.

Once the massive gateway of the " Ark "
has closed behind you, the very atmosphere seems
charged with intrigue and mystery. You cross
a narrow court-yard between the high outer wall
and the inner façade of the grim old citadel, and
plunge into a labyrinth of low passageways with
corridors that branch into the darkness on either
side. What stories of bloodshed and tyranny
these black walls and gloomy underground rooms
of the old Kajar citadel might tell! What
cruel tales of the old days when Fath Ali Shah,
" the Superb," and the conquering Nadir, ruled
Persia with a rod of iron! It is with a sigh of
relief that the visitor emerges once more into the
outer air in some interior court-yard, where even
the clamor of the Boulevard of Diamonds fails
to penetrate.

A garden filled with the sound of water,
clear as crystal, running in marble channels.
Placid fountains that ripple lazily over their

AT THE PALACE GATES

IN THE PALACE GARDENS

tiled edges, reflecting like burnished mirrors the
azure sky, the dark-foliaged trees, and the graceful arcades of the palace. A place of enchantment, a secret Garden of Delights hidden behind
the great barriers of solid masonry that surround
it. Here it is easy to imagine the veiled beauties
who graced the court of the old Persian monarchs, dragging their silken robes across the
marble pavements, among the ever-blooming
hedges of Persian roses. Yet, even in this remote spot, where the splendors of old Persia seem
to live again, the discordant note of European
" culture " has penetrated. Cast-iron stags and
greyhounds stand rigidly among the trees and
shrubbery. All about the edges of the marbled
basins where Nasr-ed-Din in his moments of
relaxation was wont to send his gayly-apparelled
courtiers to cruise in tiny models of European
ships-of-war, stand hosts of little cast-iron
statues, holding up gas-lamps of hideous European pattern.

So popular are these examples of Occidental
art that a foundry near Teheran is kept busy
supplying the demand, and every courtier with
pretensions to good taste follows this fashion in

ornamenting his garden. For, alas! Persia's advance along the paths of modern civilization has been accompanied by the same decay of artistic taste that marks the new epoch in Japan and India. Fancy a nation of artists with a secret admiration for plug hats and claw-hammer coats! And while Persia is being ransacked for the few remaining treasures of her ancient art that have not yet been exported to ornament the palaces of American millionnaires, your Persian gentleman collects with perhaps as much discrimination American clocks, German lithographs, and " articles de Paris," the latter for the most part manufactured by the wily Muscovite in St. Petersburg and Odessa.

The Treasure House or Museum is a series of rooms in a distant wing of the Palace filled with countless jimcracks,—half toy, half treasure,—such as only the Oriental mind could conceive of, or covet. To reach it you must pass through more interminable corridors, through more silent court-yards and across deserted suites of musty apartments filled with stiff, ungraceful European furniture, chipped and broken by long journeys on camel-back across the Persian desert.

On the walls hang pictures by Persian artists, copied from European models (often by an odd freak of Oriental taste exact duplicates of each other), cheap German lithographs, and an occasional canvas of real value presented by some foreign ruler.

The Treasure House itself at the first glance appears to be a veritable Aladdin's cave, and further inspection leaves the visitor filled with wonder at the incongruous treasures it contains. Side by side with the loot of the richest provinces of India, brought here by the conquering Nadir, stand the oddly-assorted purchases made in London and Paris by the late Shah and his father—a collection of umbrellas, knives, forks, combs, and other articles of common use in Europe, kept in glass cases, each article neatly labelled and set out in orderly array for the instruction and astonishment of the stay-at-homes. Next to a self-playing piano stands a terrestrial globe made of precious stones, the seas mapped in sapphires and the continents in rubies and emeralds. By the side of a phonograph with a repertory of " rag-time " melodies, is placed a Chinese vase of blue porcelain six feet high at least, and worth a king's ransom.

The guide shows you carved and inlaid chests, where, a few years ago, the Shah's visitors were invited to plunge their arms to the elbow in heaps of pearls from the Persian Gulf and turquoise from the Imperial mines, although (perhaps for this very reason) they stand empty to-day.

On the walls hang rich carpets, and prayer-rugs hallowed by the devotions of Persian Kings and Heroes. Weapons of the days of Shah Abbas are hung side by side with the latest pattern of European fire-arms—shot-guns, their stocks and barrels covered with precious stones; and small cannon, mounted with solid gold, that run on wheels of carved rosewood.

Perhaps the most interesting object in this collection of strange wonders is the famous Peacock Throne, brought by the conquering Persian armies from the sack of Delhi. Following Eastern traditions, the Peacock Throne is built in the form of a tall coach or sofa whereon the monarch reclines in state while dispensing justice. Every inch of its surface is covered with thin plates of solid gold, elaborately chased and enamelled in brilliant colors. The two jewelled birds that give the throne its name (with a little stretch of the imagination they may very well pass for peacocks) hold in their golden beaks a sunburst of diamonds, which a clock-work mechanism concealed at the back causes to revolve with dazzling effect. It is strange to reflect that beneath this brilliant bauble once reclined the terrible Mogul Emperor of India, Shah Jehan, who built the marble Taj, and Jehangir the Magnificent, when they dispensed the wide sway of their royal justice in the golden pavilion that crowns the great sandstone fortress in far-away Delhi.

One of the most interesting of our experiences was an audience with " The Threshold of the Universe," one of the least of the exalted titles by which the late ruler of Persia, Muzaffar-ed-Din, was always officially styled. A note brought to the American Legation by one of the mace-bearers from the Palace informed us that the hour for this momentous event had been fixed at " one hour before sunset " on Christmas Day.

At the " Gate of the Ambassadors " we

were met by a dozen or more of the Shah's running footmen dressed in broad-skirted coats of scarlet cloth, wearing oddly-shaped caps with an arrangement of feathers that recalled the crest of a cockatoo, rising for more than three feet above their heads. Preceded by these gorgeous individuals walking in solemn procession, we were led through an interminable labyrinth of corridors and passageways to the royal anteroom. This we found filled with waiting courtiers and attendants, while a detachment of the Palace Guards in red coats, blue breeches, and high top boots presented arms vigorously as we entered.

European Ambassadors in the early days of the nineteenth century, when Persia was still rarely visited by foreigners, have left amusing accounts of the struggle that took place, on the occasion of every audience, between Persian Court etiquette and European ideas of what is dignified and becoming. Until within the last few years all who were granted the inestimable privilege of entering the Royal presence were required to don high red leggings of a peculiar cut, which concealed their nether limbs from the

AN AUDIENCE WITH THE LATE SHAH

august gaze, unless indeed they chose to appear
in the flowing garments of the Orient.

Morier has described in his immortal "Hadji
Baba" the appearance of the European Ambassadors in the eyes of the Persian Court in
the beginning of the last century. " The Franks
with their unhidden legs, their coats cut to the
quick, and their unbearded chins, looked like
birds moulting, or diseased apes, or anything but
human creatures, when compared with the splen-
didly-dressed persons by whom they were surrounded." And it is to be feared that this un-
flattering view of our customs and apparel is
still held by a large majority of the Shah's
subjects.

But the old régime, the vizirs in flowing
robes and jewelled turbans who once ruled at the
Court of Teheran, have long since passed away.
Incongruous as it may seem, the Persian officials
now follow the fashions of London and Paris,
and in the capital of Persia the once despised
frock coat of the infidel may even be said to play
a political rôle, for it distinguishes the more
progressive members of the Court party from
the conservative lower classes of the town, who,

for the most part, cling to the picturesque apparel of their ancestors.

Most of the officials present in the anteroom on the occasion of our reception wore European Court dress or uniforms, and glittered with the stars and crosses of foreign orders. Some of the older courtiers wore the highest Persian decorations, a portrait of the Shah, set with diamonds, hanging from a broad green ribbon about their necks. Many of the younger officials spoke French among themselves, and no Court of Europe could have outdone them in decorum and rigid politeness.

When our turn came to pass into the Royal presence, an official dressed in a splendid robe of old Cashmere embroidery, thrown over an ordinary suit of evening clothes, led us through a double file of the Palace Guard stationed before a carved and inlaid doorway, into a large, sunny room, where we found the Shah awaiting our coming. His Majesty was plainly dressed in a dark blue coat, with the broad golden epaulets of a general officer of the Persian army. The Royal egrett clasped by a famous diamond was set in the front of his black astrakhan hat, but with that exception he wore no insignia or decoration of any kind.

While the flowery and tedious compliments that Persian Court etiquette exacts were being exchanged through the medium of our interpreters his Majesty, whose health was already undermined by the malady that eventually caused his death, stood leaning impatiently on a gold-headed cane, and the officials had hardly finished their sonorous Persian salutations when he addressed us directly in French, which he spoke slowly but correctly.

After expressing his pleasure at seeing visitors who had come so far with the sole intention of visiting Persia, the Shah spoke of his last trip to Europe and compared the comforts of travelling there with the difficulties that exist in his own kingdom.

" The next time you visit Persia, I hope you will be able to travel from one end of the country to the other as easily and safely as in Europe. My Ministers and I are especially interested in developing a system of railways for Persia.

" Railways are the secret of European

progress. We have in this country many
natural resources which must await a railway to
make them available. I should especially like to
see foreign capitalists interested in our Persian
mines and oil-fields. If it were not for the dangers of a sea voyage I should visit America and
see its wonders for myself. The sea, however,
has a most pernicious influence on my health."

The Shah paused and seemed brooding over
some painful memory of the past.

"If a voyage of only a few hours across
the English Channel could so affect me, how
can I hope ever to reach your far-off land
alive?"

I attempted to explain to his Majesty that
sea-sickness is at worst a temporary disorder,
but I could see that the Royal mind was firmly
made up on this point, and even his interest in
the great Republic of Yankidonia (which oddly
enough is the Persian equivalent for "New
World") would never tempt him to visit a continent not to be reached on *terra firma.*

While our interview was prolonged beyond
the ordinary limits by the Shah's wish to honor
visitors from the "far-away Republic," our

further conversation concerned matters hardly worth recording. We found his Majesty much interested in photography, and he examined the apparatus we had brought with almost boyish delight and appreciation. He directed, himself, the grouping of his retinue for a series of " snapshots," and it is to his skill in the art of photography that I am indebted for the views of the Palace accompanying this chapter.

During his two journeys to Europe the late Shah's purchases in London and Paris were the delight and amazement of the shop-keepers. Throughout these trips he showed a truly Royal interest in cameras, phonographs, musical boxes, automobiles, and almost every kind of expensive mechanical novelty. Nor were the members of the Royal suite content until they had mastered the delicate mechanism of these infidel inventions, sometimes with disastrous results. The collection of modern weapons and fire-arms kept at the " Ark " is one of the most complete in the world, and the traveller who brought with him as a gift some new pattern of rifle or revolver was sure of a hearty welcome. One of Muzaffar-ed-Din's favorite amusements was firing at a mark with a battery of small cannon, and the prize he carried off in a pistol match near Paris was doubtless one of the pleasantest recollections of his last European trip. Like most of the Kajar princes, he was devoted to the chase, and the Royal preserves at Teheran were kept constantly stocked with all kinds of wild game for the pleasure of the Royal hunting-parties.

In spite of these frivolities Muzaffar-ed-Din left his mark on the history of his country. Although the late Shah was pleased to call himself a conservative, his general policy was one of reform. Indeed the present ascendency of the Liberal party in Persia owes much to his friendly attitude in the beginning of the movement. Besides his active interest in developing the resources of Persia, he was responsible for many reforms in the administration of justice and the management of Persian finances. While the latter branch of the public service still leaves everything to be desired—notably in the collection of taxes and other revenues of the state—we no longer hear of the accused in Persian courts of law being buried in quicklime, or having their eyes burned out, as in the " good old days."

MOHAMMED ALI MIRZA, SHAH OF PERSIA

And while the bastinado still remains a feature of Persian legal procedure, its use is restricted to certain classes of offenders.

The Vali-Ahd or heir apparent was not in Teheran at the time of our visit, as according to Persian custom the prince destined to succeed to the throne is kept at a distance from the centre of Court life and intrigue, and rarely visits the capital during the lifetime of the sovereign. It was a great concession to modern ideas when the present Shah, Mohammed Ali Mirza, was summoned from Tabriz, and called upon to act as regent before the death of his father, Muzaffar-ed-Din. Little is known outside of Persia of the character or capabilities of the young ruler. As Governor of Tabriz, near the Russian border, he was at one time reported to be wholly under the influence of Russian advisers, but after the revolutionary outbreak in the Caucasus he rid himself very summarily of a crowd of Russian adventurers who hung about his Court, and commenced to show a more friendly feeling towards the English officials in Teheran.

In all likelihood Mohammed Ali Mirza's

some lad whose pleasing manners made a favorable impression on those present.

Shortly after the coronation the personal entourage of the new ruler moved into the Palace, taking the places and apartments of the horde of petty officials and domestics who had gathered about the late Muzaffar-ed-Din in his declining years. These new favorites included a Russian doctor, a foreign interpreter (also Russian), and the Russian tutor attached to the person of the Crown Prince. The late Shah's English physician, who stood high in the favor of Muzaffar-ed-Din, was retained. Needless to say, the young Shah's choice of his household and advisers was watched with a jealous eye by the diplomatic representatives of the great powers at Teheran, but he seems to have avoided giving offense to any of the foreign influences that play such an important rôle in Persian politics.

Since the signing of the Anglo-Russian *entente,* regulating the affairs and interests of those two countries, Persia's external troubles are for the moment abated or postponed. On the other hand, questions that never before confronted an Oriental ruler beset the young mon-

arch on every hand. To steer a course between
the contending dangers of a reactionary movement led by the Palace officials anxious to
preserve the old autocracy's privileges and the
socialistic measures proposed by the advanced
party in Parliament, would be a difficult task
for a far more experienced statesman. To
judge from his general policy, the present Shah
is something of an opportunist, ready to throw
the weight and influence of the Royal preroga-
tive on the side of whichever party or clique
happens to be in the ascendant, and in the present
state of Persian affairs this is doubtless the
wisest course to pursue. From his natural advisers, the officials and dignitaries of his Court
—certainly since the untimely death of the Sadre
Azam—he can hope for but little assistance.
These worthies are said to view with almost
comical dismay the curtailing of their old privileges by a popular assembly, and their whole
attitude towards the new Parliament reminds one
of the ancient Eastern tale of the unfortunate
Magician, who by his arts was able to summon
powerful spirits from the deep, but forgot the
magic words that gave him control of their

superhuman powers. The Genius of Democracy
evoked by the late Shah's love of modern forms
—if not of modern institutions—now towers
over his successor, and Persia after three thousand years of despotism is for the present, at
least, the most liberally governed among the
native states of the Orient.

V.

THE traveller on his arrival in Teheran soon learns to make allowance for much that while Occidental in form still remains very Oriental in fact. The European trips of Shah Nasr-ed-Din and his successor were a tremendous step in the eyes of their contemporaries. The innovations they brought back from Europe, even to-day, are little to the taste of the great majority of their more conservative countrymen whose opinion of the relative importance of Persia and the foreign countries beyond her borders is aptly expressed by the quaint preamble to the treaty which still governs our relations with the Shah's realm. This document has for its high contracting parties on the one hand, " The President of the United States," and on the other, " His Majesty as exalted as the Planet Saturn; the Sovereign to whom the Sun serves as a Standard; whose Splendor and Magnificence are equal to that of the Skies; the Sublime Sovereign; the Monarch whose Armies are as the Stars," etc. And to

the older generation of Persians, the sight of
their monarch consorting on terms of equality
with the infidel potentates of less fortunate lands
is a spectacle to be viewed with pious horror and
aversion.

On the other hand, among the Court officials
one finds a tendency to somewhat indiscrimi-
nately admire the things and ways of Europe.
This is especially true of those who have themselves enjoyed the advantages of foreign travel,
and for some years it has been the custom of the
Shah's Government to send abroad every year a
number of young men chosen among the sons
of the Persian nobility, to be instructed in
European schools and universities.

But in spite of his fear of being considered
fanatique the Persian Court official still retains
the prejudices of his forefathers. The veneer of
European culture in most cases does not extend
far below the surface.   Were it not for his im-
maculate Bond Street tailoring (although he
would probably scorn to admit it) many a young
noble who ornaments the Shah's Palace, could
still sit for hours squatting on his heels, or sleep
comfortably at night with nothing but a Kurdish

rug between his person and the hard floor. Above all he has retained the old ideas as to his rights and prerogatives. He continues to feel it his duty to find places at Court for all his relations, so that often whole families down to the youngest children are drawing salaries from the public treasury. He still considers his tenants and peasantry, in the old feudal spirit, as created for the convenience and benefit of his class, and from his European experiences (except in a few notable cases) he has profited but little—unless we consider his modern clothes, and the ability to speak a little French or English, as a distinct gain to his country.

The strong nationalistic spirit that marks the new era in Persian affairs is one of the most interesting features of the present movement in Persia. It is not among the frock-coated European dandies of the Court that we must look for the men who are now taking the leading part in the new agitation for Reform. Many of the Constitutionalist leaders wear the flowing robes and white turban of the Mohammedan priesthood. Recently the Liberal Parliament by an overwhelming majority voted to suppress the publication of a Teheran newspaper which had dared to propose the substitution of a new civil code modelled on European lines for the old common law based on the precepts of the Koran. One of the chief causes of popular complaint against the leaders of the Court party is their subserviency to foreign influences and their un-patriotic policy of importing foreign officials into Persia, notably in the case of the customs administration.

Following the ill-fated " social revolution " in the Caucasus, events in Persia advanced at a rapid pace, and the demands of the new Liberal party and the more enlightened inhabitants of Teheran brought about unheard-of changes in the time-honored methods of government. With all his zeal for European forms of procedure, it is unlikely that the late Shah or his father ever dreamed of any radical departure from the old paternal rule of the Sovereign, and the idea that the complicated machinery of state created to impress the Courts of Europe with their progressive views, might ever be called upon to operate, certainly never entered the minds of their advisers. Even after the failure of the

Liberals in the neighboring Russian provinces,
the popular party was loud in its demands that
some of the " reforms " and voluntary concessions made during the past ten years by the
Persian government should be put to a practical
test. The conservative clergy of Teheran em-
braced the opportunity of associating themselves
with this patriotic demand, and brought matters
to a crisis in July, 1906, by means of a " general
strike " which for a time threatened to seriously
hamper the administration of justice throughout
Persia—the latter, as in all Mohammedan countries, being founded on the interpretation of the
Sacred Writings.

The Mutjehids, or religious law-givers, at
one time started in a body for the sacred city
of Kerbela as a protest against the fashion in
which their advice and demands were ignored
by the Court party; and had already proceeded
for some distance on their way before the latter
were constrained to relent. In the meanwhile,
the Liberal leaders in Teheran, fearing the vengeance of the troops in the pay of the Government, had taken refuge in the compound of the
British Legation, where according to treaty

OLD PERSIAN JUSTICE—THE BASTINADO

rights they were safe against arrest or persecution. It was reported at the time that no less than 18,000 inhabitants of Teheran had thus thrown themselves on the mercy of a foreign government.

Alarmed by this determined though pacific resistance, and by the sympathetic attitude of a large part of the population, the late Shah's advisers at last decided to yield, and a manifesto was issued in the name of Muzaffar-ed-Din calling for a *duma,* or popular assembly. The document summoning the first Persian Parliament was worded as follows:

"The Shah, since his accession to the throne, has always had the intention to introduce real and efficient reforms in all the departments of the state, so as to further the well-being of his people. For this purpose his Majesty has now decided that a National Council shall be formed at Teheran, composed of representatives of the Kajar princes (the royal tribe), clergy, nobles, merchants, and tradesmen. These representatives will be elected by their peers. The National Council shall deliberate on all important affairs of state, and shall have the power and right to express its views with freedom and full confidence in regard to all reforms which may be necessary to the welfare of the country. The result of the deliberations of the Council shall be submitted through the intermediary of the First Minister of State to the Shah for his Majesty's signature and shall then be carried into effect. The rules of procedure of the National Council shall be drawn up with the approval of the members and shall receive the Shah's signature. The Council, after determining its rules of procedure, shall then begin to give effect to the sacred laws of Islam and to introduce the necessary reforms."

Thus was accomplished, by an almost bloodless revolution, the same laudable ends that ended in disastrous failure after months of rapine and outrage just across the border in " civilized " and " Christian " Russia! Certainly an encouraging and instructive sign of the march of events in the " Awakening East."

The first official act of the Vali-Ahd when summoned to take over the reins of government during the late Shah's fatal illness, was to assure himself of the support of the new popular Assembly. The revised Constitution of January First, signed by the dying hand of Muzaffar-ed-Din was ratified by the present monarch, and the principle of popular government became an acknowledged part of Persian administration.

The first Persian National Convention was made up of delegates from all over Persia, but most came from the Northern provinces, where constant contact with the restless population of the Caucasus had familiarized the people with the principles of liberty and popular government. While not elected by popular suffrage, this body undoubtedly represented the will of the more enlightened and progressive inhabitants of the country, especially in the great centers of population, Tabriz, Teheran, and Ispahan.

The confusion of parties and policies long prevented all other business but voluble and fruitless debates, while tirades directed against the Shah's Ministers took up most of the time of the Assembly. Forgetting that in the beginning, at least, royal toleration was responsible for the rapid spread of the Liberal movement, the Par-

liament seemed bent on forcing an open rupture
with the Palace. But the Shah's policy of conciliation, and the advice of the late Atabek Azam,
his Minister of State, averted a dangerous
crisis, and by timely concessions made to the
demands of the radical members the inevitable
struggle between the Constitutionalists and the
Anti-Constitutionalists, or Court party, was
postponed.

The first efforts of the National Assembly
were directed towards securing from the Shah's
advisers the assurance that they would be properly represented in the formation of the new
Imperial Cabinet, which still retained the ad-
ministrative functions of the government. The
Government further acceded to popular demands
by dismissing the Belgian officials in charge of
the customs administration, and the leaders of
the Reform movement next turned their attention to the crying abuses of the provincial gov-
ernorships. This was a popular as well as a
patriotic move, and materially strengthened their
influence in the Southern provinces, where the
workings and propaganda of the secret societies
who are at the back of the progressive element in

Parliament had not penetrated. The crowning success of their crusade was the recall of the famous Zil-es-Sultan from the governorship of Ispahan, which he had held for the last thirty-eight years. This remarkable man, an uncle of the late Shah, has been frequently called the most accomplished and powerful of the Kajar princes. At one time he was able to extend his power until he became the virtual ruler of nearly one-half of the Imperial domain. His army, modelled on European lines, was considered by foreign observers the most effective body of troops in Persia. Of late years his power had been on the wane, but his recall, associated with that of other reactionary governors, was none the less a noteworthy triumph for the leaders of the National movement.

Taking into account the extraordinary circumstances that made the first National Assembly a possibility, and the apathy of by far the greater number of the Shah's subjects where their personal liberties are concerned, the work accomplished by the Persian Parliament after a little more than a year of existence, is noteworthy and promising. As in past years, the financial condition of the kingdom leaves much to be desired. The Minister of Finance during his short tenure of office having accumulated a debt of more than $700,000 (which in the total absence of foreign credit was distributed among local creditors), recently gave up his portfolio in despair and asked to be relieved of his functions. Parliament, equal to the emergency, refused to accept his resignation, and sent him back to wrestle with the time-honored problem: making zero revenue = a constantly-increasing expenditure. The Shah's entourage have succeeded in shifting to the shoulders of the people's representatives the constantly-recurring question of how to raise revenue with every natural resource long since hypothecated in favor of foreign creditors. It must be remembered, however, that Persia's unfortunate financial situation is largely the result of the follies and extravagances of a previous régime, and the present misfortunes that threaten the credit of the country have their root in reckless borrowing and improvidence lasting over a period of twenty years or more.

Hopeful signs of internal improvement are

noticeable all over Persia, especially in the Northern provinces, where the towns and villages have taken steps to form local municipal assemblies modelled on European lines. Attempts are being made in many provinces to inaugurate a fair system of taxation, and the people are beginning to realize that the passing of the iniquitous system of tax " farming " means the beginning of a new era of prosperity for the poor as well as the rich.

Among other signs of the awakening interest of Persian people in the affairs of their country is the sudden and remarkable growth of the Persian press. In place of the old " Moniteur Official," Teheran can now boast of no less than four daily and thirty weekly papers. Most of these are rabidly progressive in their tone, nor can their influence be said to be wholly beneficial to the cause they support. Nevertheless, it is a promising sign that the absolute apathy towards public affairs which was a characteristic trait only a few years ago, is giving place to a new sense of social responsibility.

In the old days the administration of Teheran was composed of but two high officials, who interpreted the edicts and carried out the will of their Sovereign Lord and Master. These were the Grand Vizir and the High Treasurer. When the first Persian Constitution went into effect—an idea brought back from Europe by Nasr-ed-Din, and for a long time but vaguely understood by the great majority of his subjects —the system of government was recast along European lines. A Council of Ministers, numbering no less than thirty in all, was supposed to assist the Shah in his deliberations. These dignitaries were rarely, if ever, convened, and in many cases their salaries were diverted to other purposes. Indeed, until the meeting of the recent popular Assembly, the practical workings of the Persian administration remained very nearly as before, in the hands of a few Palace officials and favorite Ministers of the Shah.

The present monarch was fortunate in having as an adviser, during the first critical months of his reign, one of the ablest statesmen in the Orient. This remarkable man, Ali Akbar Khan, better known by his title of Atabek Azam, made himself almost indispensable to three successive shahs, and for twenty years guided the ship of

THE ATABEK AZAM

AN ORIENTAL STATESMAN—THE LATE ATABEK AZAM

state through the troubled waters of Middle Eastern diplomacy. Indeed his whole life was literally passed in the public service, for he was born in the precincts of the Royal Palace, where his father occupied the post of cup-bearer or wine-taster to the present Shah's grandfather—an old Biblical office that still exists at the Persian Court. But in spite of his early training as a courtier, the late Grand Vizir was far from being the typical Oriental statesman, as most people imagine that person to be.

During an extended interview I was impressed with his knowledge of European affairs, and especially with his understanding of the conditions that prevail in America. Indeed in appearance and manner the Atabek Azam was curiously like the best type of the American " business man," although professedly unable to speak any other language than his native Persian. He is said to have gained the confidence of the Kajar rulers by a mixture of diplomacy and a frankness little less than appalling to the sensibilities of the smooth-tongued sycophants who surround the Peacock Throne. On several occasions this gift of telling unpleasant truths gained for him the resentment and displeasure of the Sovereign, and during his long career he was more than once stripped of his office, only to be recalled each time to enjoy new favors and higher honors. During one of these recent periods of exile he visited the principal cities of the United States, and on his return to Persia became (until his untimely death in August, 1907,) the arbiter between the reactionary Court party and the more conservative element in the Liberal Parliament.

During my visit to Teheran, his Highness summoned me to his house, where he asked me innumerable questions as to the easiest manner of reaching America and the probable reception of a Persian mission. He said:

"My policy as regards Persia has always had as its key-note to avoid entangling alliances with neighboring states. Persia must look far afield for the support of a disinterested ally, and I should like to see the closest relations existing between the Shah's Government and the people of your great Republic. America's advance into the Orient, and your policy of the 'open door,' have made a profound impression among East-

AT THE HOUSE OF THE MUSHIR-ED-DOWLEH

(THE PRESENT HEAD OF THE COURT PARTY)

ern people. With the growth of your Oriental
trade you will be forced to interest yourself in
the affairs of Persia, for with the coming of rail-
roads, and the development of our natural resources our country will again take its place
among the great commercial nations of the
world."

It is probable his visit to the United States
made a powerful impression on this clever Oriental statesman. In any case it is certain that on
his return to office his old devotion to autocratic
forms was considerably modified, and he was one
of the few officials of the old régime to exercise
any appreciable influence on the course of recent events.

Since the dastardly murder of the Atabek
Azam at the hands of a Socialist fanatic, the
Mushir-ed-Dowleh has once more become the
chief adviser of the Shah. The present Grand
Vizir has long held the post of Minister of
Foreign Affairs, and is noted for his conciliatory
spirit. The popularity of his predecessors was
gravely compromised by their subserviency to
Russia, and by pandering to the extravagances

of the officials who surround the Sovereign.
With the weakening of Russian prestige and the
growth of the Liberal party an entirely new
policy must be adopted. The Mushir-ed-Dowleh
apparently possesses the qualifications needed to
meet the situation, as he is said to have the confidence of the priesthood and the " Conservative "
element, as well as that of the more liberal merchants of Teheran.

I remember him at the time of my visit, a
kindly gentleman of the old Persian school, who
made up for his ignorance of European languages by a great urbanity and gentleness of
manner. During our visit to his house in
Teheran I noticed especially its atmosphere of
sturdy conservatism, and the absence of many
signs of a mistaken European culture that one
meets with in the homes of most Court officials.
Our interview, carried on through the medium
of an interpreter, was marked by all the personal
questions that old Persian courtesy demands, and
while we did not touch on any matters of political
interest, I was impressed by his strong good
sense and general information about foreign
lands.

Although the Grand Vizir still holds an important place in the Persian administration, since the last political "shake up" the real head of the Cabinet is said to be Saad-ed-Dowleh, who holds the portfolio of Foreign Affairs. He virtually controls the "working majority" in Parliament (whenever that very intangible part of the National Assembly is able to make itself apparent), and his appointment is another triumph for the Liberal party. True to his policy of conciliation, the Shah, following the demands of the Parliament leaders, has dismissed all the more reactionary members of his former Cabinet, and the present government is for the first time in actual sympathy and touch with the progressive leaders of the Reform movement.

VI.

NOT far from our lodgings in Teheran, in
the shadow of the high walls that surround the
British Legation, the curious order of religious
mendicants known throughout the Middle East
under the general name of " darvish," had established their meeting place.   On the lonely paths
that cross the Persian desert, as well as in the
crowded market-places of her great cities, similar
rendezvous are to be found where members of
this mysterious brotherhood gather together to
discuss their strange affairs.   Almost every day
we would see some new recruit join the council-
fire—wild-eyed smokers of hemp and bhang,
their ragged garments stained with the dust of
far countries—who rested a few days among
their comrades; then, their adventures told,
passed on their way to some new place of
pilgrimage.

The rules that govern the conduct of this
strange brotherhood will doubtless remain a
mystery to Europeans.   Religious free-thinkers,

A YOUNG DARVISH

THE BEGGAR CHIEF

at odds with all the restraints imposed by the
laws of Mohammed, they profess at the same
time to be the corner-stone of Islam. Their
ranks are recruited from all classes of society.
The merchant, tired of business, or the vizir
wearied by the cares of statecraft, will take up
the darvish begging-bowl and wander forth in
search of that contentment which is found in
absolute irresponsibility. The darvish who asks
your alms may be the lord of a hundred villages,
or merely some idle apprentice too indolent to
earn an honest living at home.

By the common people they are half feared
as possessing strange knowledge and occult
powers, half despised for their dissolute habits
and unorthodox ways of life. The poorest bazar
porter will gladly share his daily pittance at the
insolent demand of one of these half-sacred
mendicants, in return for his prayers and inter-
cessions at some distant shrine, and a moment
later laugh with you at darvish jugglery and
tricks. Háfiz in his famous book " Concerning
Darvishs " has many shrewd things to say of the
practices of these self-asserting saints, yet the

hold that their pretensions have on the Eastern mind is not to be denied.

To properly understand the Persian character, it is necessary to realize what an important part his religious beliefs play in the routine of his every-day life. Just outside of the gates of Teheran stands a group of ruined buildings that represent all that remains of one of the most considerable foreign enterprises ever attempted in Persia. Here, a Belgian company undertook, a few years ago, to establish a refinery for the manufacture of beet-root sugar, under conditions that warranted every hope of success. All of the sugar used in such quantities by the Persians to flavor their favorite " tchai " is now brought from a great distance on the backs of camels and other pack-animals, and as this perishable commodity lends itself with difficulty to such modes of transport, the price is proportionately high. The land around Teheran is easily adapted to the culture of beet-root, and for some time a new and important industry promised to benefit the peasants of the neighborhood. At first the affairs of the company flourished and the promoters and stockholders in distant Europe began to congratulate themselves on their investment. But within a few weeks there came a sudden and unaccountable falling off in the demand, and at last the native customers ceased buying the sugar from the new mills. The reason was not far to seek. Either some emissary from the white-turbaned mollahs in a neighboring shrine had been sent away empty handed, or some religious caprice had moved the priesthood to a Holy War on the products of the " unbeliever," for the sugar manufactured by the Belgian company was declared " unclean " and classed with pork and other abominations not fit to pass the lips of the Faithful. For months the official in charge attempted to cope with local prejudice, but all in vain. At the present day the rusting machinery and empty windows of an expensive plant bear a mute testimonial to the power of old ideals even in " The Awakening East."

Contrary to what is very generally believed, fire-worship ceased to be the national religion of Persia many centuries ago. In remote corners of the Shah's empire the sacred flame still burns, tended in secret by humble worshippers who have preserved the symbol, if not the pure faith, of Ahura Mazda. A few miserable "Guebers" may still be found worshipping the volcanic fires that rise from the earth near the oil-fields of Baku, and in India the Parsis—Persians of the old faith—who took refuge there before the all-conquering armies of Islam, still observe the precepts of the Zendavesta. But though the Sun still figures with the Lion on the Imperial arms of Persia, the old faith is dead, and the altars of the great Spirit of Good, whom the ancient Jews recognized as one with their Jehovah, are broken and deserted.

With few exceptions the Persians of to-day are Mohammedans of the Shiah sect. This great division of the Mohammedan faith differs from the Sunni or orthodox Mohammedans in that they recognize the claims of Ali, the son-in-law of the Prophet, to be his legitimate successor to the honors of the Califate, and believe that the succession to the high office was divinely transmitted through the members of his family in the persons of a series of saints called Imams. The tombs of these Imams are found scattered all over Persia, and are always reverenced as holy places of pilgrimage. The Persians have es-

THE HOUR OF PRAYER

poused the wrongs of Ali and his martyred children, making of them a grievance against the rest of Islam; confounding the Sunni, together with Christian and Jew, in a universal doctrine of hatred and contempt.

To a Persian, religion enters into the minutest detail of every-day life. Not only does it prescribe what he shall eat and drink, how he shall stand and sit, how he must rise in the morning, and how he must retire again at night, but even after death his poor body must be carried far from the familiar scenes among which he has passed his existence, to be buried among strangers in the holy ground that surrounds the shrine of some saintly Imam.

In the cities of Persia one meets at every turn the Mohammedan priest or mollah. His flowing robes gathered about him to escape the pollution of a Christian's touch, he passes with lowering looks and a muttered curse on the unbeliever and all his works. The special mark of his office is a great white turban worn in place of the astrakhan cap affected by the great majority of his fellow countrymen. Often this mushroom-like head-piece will be of dark blue or green cloth, showing that its wearer claims relationship with the family of the Prophet. In Persia these " seyids " are so numerous that one meets them in the humblest walks of life. But even the hamal or porter who wears a wisp of green cloth about his ragged cap, claims some consideration and perhaps a few extra coppers as well from the True Believer, on account of the drop of sacred blood that runs in his veins.

Shortly after our arrival in Teheran there commenced the great Mohammedan feast of " Ramazan," which in Persia is kept with especial strictness and solemnity. For a month the whole life of the city takes on a changed aspect. From the moment when the firing of a cannon near the Palace at the first rays of dawn signals the beginning of the fast, till another at sunset announces its close, not a drop of water nor a morsel of food may pass the lips of a True Believer. Even the solace he might derive from tobacco, the ubiquitous kalian or water-pipe, is denied him.

During the day a strange silence reigns over the whole city. In the bazars most of the shops remain tightly shuttered, and the few people one

A MOLLAH

meets abroad in the streets have their faces drawn
and pinched by hunger. Even the most Euro-
peanized of the Court officials will refrain from
joining in the traditional cup of tea or coffee,
which, in Persia, must be offered on the occasion
of every social visit.

But this period of fasting, instituted by the
Prophet that the poor might benefit by the
privations of the rich, has become in reality a
period of feasting and debauchery. At night
the streets, which in ordinary times are dark and
silent soon after sunset, are lighted by torches
and filled with a busy crowd seeking entertainment or going about their affairs. All the pro-
vision shops about the city are open once more,
and do a rushing business among crowds of
hungry customers, while from every house comes
the sound of feasting and revelry. Jugglers,
dancing boys (called luti) and singing women
ply their trade, while ram-fighting and enter-
tainments of an even more doubtful character
are given by generous hosts to their less fortunate
friends all over the city; and the whole population gives itself over to enjoyment until the
ominous boom of the morning gun once more

warns them to seek refuge from the pangs of hunger in sleep which lasts throughout the day.

"Moharram," the great fast in honor of the martyrdom of the children of Ali, is, however, observed by the Persians with great severity. It is then that the peculiar fanaticism of the Shiah's belief finds its most violent expression. While the fast is kept with more or less rigor throughout the Moslem world, in Persia it reaches the dignity of a national ceremony— a period of universal mourning and expiation, during which the wrongs and sufferings of the Prophet's family at the time of their persecution, more than a thousand years ago, are recalled and lamented as though they were of yesterday— and more real tears are shed for the martyrs of Kerbela than would fall at the death of some near and beloved relative.

In every town of Persia the scenes of this pious martyrdom are reënacted in elaborate processions and plays, where the parts of the sacred personages concerned are taken by the highest and worthiest in the land. In Teheran a great iron structure has been built, which is used but once a year, to present this sacred tragedy before the Court officials, who assemble to witness the edifying spectacle and to express their grief by the most violent lamentations.

Travellers who have witnessed this peculiar religious representation declare that the faith displayed renders it touching in the extreme. The actors are men and boys well drilled in their parts by months of study and preparation. The story that they tell,—the brutal murder of men, women, and children, the noblest in Islam, by an implacable and relentless usurper, among the burning sands of the Euphrates desert,—is touching in itself, and the language, consecrated by years of tradition, is free from the ridiculous hyperbole of the modern Persian. Tears flow from the eyes of the spectators and groans of unfeigned sorrow fill the air, while the audience or congregation are wrought to a wild pitch of grief and religious fanaticism.

In atonement for the sorrows and wrongs of Husein and his kindred, processions of white-robed penitents pass through the streets of Teheran, the more devout worshippers cutting and gashing their own flesh with long knives and sharp instruments until their snowy robes are streaming with blood.

It is at this time, too, that darvishs and other saintly mendicants reap their richest harvest from the credulous with ingenious methods of self-torture either feigned or real—lying on beds studded with iron spikes, eating live scorpions and coals of fire, or hanging themselves before their admiring audience from great hooks that pierce the flesh of the shoulders. At this time, too, the True Believer is filled with a violent hatred towards all dissenting sects, and Jews, Christians, and "Guebers" find it wise to keep away from their path. Even the members of the diplomatic corps are warned to remain as much as possible within the walls of their legations, and the foreign colony in Teheran view with some relief the arrival of the period of rejoicing that follows the fast.

The latter half of the nineteenth century witnessed the rise in Persia of the so-called "Babi Movement." A great deal of what has been written about the aims and beliefs of this sect is chiefly remarkable for its inaccuracy. What undoubtedly commenced as a semi-political movement for the reform of the Shiah Mohammedan faith throughout Persia and the Middle

A PROCESSION OF PENITENTS

East has been hailed by some writers as a religion destined to raise Persia to a higher level of civilization, and by others considered merely as the workings of a dangerous society of political revolutionists. It is not necessary to pass any judgment here on a subject which has been so generally misunderstood outside the borders of the Shah's realm. But as Babism may yet play a part in the future history of Persia, it is interesting to consider what is known of its aims and history.

Mirza Ali Mohammed, the founder of Babism, began his career as a Shakhi, one of the numerous mystical sects which have grown up within the bosom of the Mohammedan Church. About 1845 he declared himself to be the " Bab " or " Gate," through which the faithful might communicate with the " hidden Imam," a prophet or messiah who, according to Shiah beliefs, will some day appear to rule the world and establish a universal empire over mankind. The Bab, as he styled himself, soon gathered about him a band of religious and political malcontents, and other disciples attracted by the high moral tone of his teachings, many of whose tenets were borrowed from the Christian beliefs and the philosophical precepts of the older religions.

In a short time the movement began to assume such proportions that the Persian Government, urged on by the priesthood, saw fit to intervene; the Bab was imprisoned, and a fierce persecution of his followers began throughout Persia. In some places the Babists, organizing for defence, offered a determined resistance to large bodies of troops sent against them. They even captured and held several towns and strongholds in the more distant provinces, and the movement began to take on a distinctly political and revolutionary character. In 1850 the Bab was removed to Tabriz, where, after a further period of imprisonment, he was sentenced to death, with two of his principal followers. One of these recanted at the last moment under torture, but the execution of Ali Mohammed and his faithful disciple was marked by a striking incident which his followers have not failed to turn to account ever since.

This nineteenth century martyrdom was carried out near the great gate of the city by a firing party of Persian regulars. The victims were suspended from the walls of the town and a volley was fired at short range. When the smoke had cleared away the Bab was found lying uninjured at the foot of the wall, the bullets which riddled his companion's body having only served to cut the ropes that held him bound. The cry of " Miracle! " was raised by the populace, and had the " Bab " kept his presence of mind there can be no doubt that the population of Tabriz, and his executioners as well, would have flocked to his standard. Stunned by his fall, however, he did not grasp the opportunity which his extraordinary escape afforded him. A soldier, stepping forward, dealt him a blow across the head with a sword. The spell of what appeared for the moment a direct intervention of Providence was broken, and the executioners finished their task.

After the death of the " Bab," and the execution or martyrdom of his principal disciples, most of his followers fled to Turkish territory, while those who remained exercised the rites of the " Behai " in secret. Schisms and dissensions broke out among the elders of the faith. Rival members of the " Bab's " family claimed to be his rightful successor, each one declaring himself to be the only " Gate " through which the faithful might hope to pass on their road to " the higher life."

One claimant is now established at the ancient town of Acre in Syria, where he is visited by hundreds of pilgrims every year. He goes by the name of Abdul Baha Abbas Effendi, and is reported to be a man of considerable intelligence and learning.

Not the least curious and remarkable development of the Babist movement is the successful propaganda their teachers have made abroad, notably in England and the United States. The mystical and flowery writings of the Bab have been translated into several European languages, and within recent years have had a success comparable to Madame Blavatsky's celebrated crusade in favor of Buddhist beliefs. Babist teachers, picturesquely robed in the garb of the Orient, have travelled all over Europe and the United States, and a number of wealthy and influential converts have rewarded their efforts. The teachings of the Babist faith and the writings of the " Master " appear to be based on the broad principles of morality which are shared in common by the great religions of the world. These are dressed in a mystical language, which leaves a wide scope for the interpretations of the faithful. Unlike the Mohammedan religion, the " Behai " give to women a prominent place in their councils, and a number of prophetesses are to be found among the saints and martyrs of the new creed.

In Persia to-day, although the Babists are regarded with much suspicion by the authorities, there has been no active persecution on the part of the Government for some years. They are said still to possess a very large secret following among all classes, including a few of the higher Persian officials, and prominent members of the new Parliament. The power exerted by a great secret society whose members are further bound together by a common religious belief is certainly to be reckoned with, and the development of Babism will be followed with interest by students of Middle Eastern affairs.

VII.

IT would be hard to find a more desolate stretch of country than that lying between Teheran and the Holy City of Kum. Our road lies across a stony desert covered with snowy patches of shining salt; and all about us rise bare peaks and ridges of rock that mark the old craters of extinct volcanoes. The lunar landscape, lighted by the pale light of the earth's rays, must present just such scenes as those through which we are marching. The silence of death lies on the whole land, and after nightfall we can hear the clanging camel-bells of an approaching caravan long before the weird file of shaggy, laden beasts come swinging towards us out of the darkness.

The first night after leaving Teheran we halted at a mud caravansary set without shelter on the slope of a bleak hill-side. A caravan of camels had taken shelter in the lee of the building to escape the bitter winds, and all night long the uneasy creatures moaned and bubbled under

KUM—THE BURIAL PLACE OF IMAM REZA'S SISTER

our windows. These mournful sounds and the loud barking of the caravan dogs at first kept us wide awake, but worn out by our long ride in the open air, we nevertheless managed to snatch a few hours' sleep before sunrise, when the inexorable Abbas awoke us with the news that our horses were waiting at the door.

Our day's march lies along the shores of the salt lake of Kum, a broad sheet of water recently formed by the silting up of a small river which flows near the city. Heavy white vapors as from some giant caldron, rise from its leaden surface and gather about the top of the bare brown hills on the opposite shore. The borders of this lake appear to be a veritable sportsman's paradise. Large flocks of ducks are flying about over the marshes, rising from the reeds with a roar of flapping wings that can be heard far away, hares and foxes frequently cross the road ahead of us, and flocks of gray pigeons wheel about over head.

By the roadside herds of goats, sheep, and camels, the property of nomad Ilyats whose black tents are pitched near by, are cropping the dry salt grass. Many of the female camels have

their young by their sides—comical babies, each
one as large as a small horse, stumbling about on
their long legs, which they have not yet learned
to manage. These herds are the only riches of
their nomad owners, and though they appear to
be grazing at will over the plain, are carefully
guarded by their herdsmen. Occasionally we
see one of these, who rises from behind some
sheltering bush to stare after us—scriptural
looking figures, muffled in long cloaks, but each
man with a good rifle slung at his shoulder, ready
for use.

On the crest of a line of low hills, where
generations of pious pilgrims have built countless stone cairns to commemorate their first sight
of the Holy City, we caught a distant view of the
shining dome of Fatmah's shrine rising over the
flat roofs of the houses of Kum. We approached the gates through fields of grain and
vegetables, then entered a mournful suburb of
ruins surrounding the inhabited portion of the
city, which has dwindled to a narrow quarter of
mean houses in the neighborhood of the shrine.

The mosque of Fatmah, sister of the famous
Imam Reza, who lies buried at Meshed, is one

KUM—THE GREAT CEMETERY

of the finest specimens of religious architecture
in Persia. It stands among miserable dwellings that encompass it on every side, seeming
strangely out of keeping with their squalor and
decay. A graceful arched gateway of deep blue
Kashan tile gives access to a court-yard, around
which are grouped the buildings and porticos of
the mosque. Over the nave which covers the
tomb of the saint rises a graceful tulip-shaped
dome covered with plates of shining gold, whose
polished surface reflects the graceful outlines of
two slender minarets of the same rich blue faience
as the gateway. Behind the mosque stand two
more high minarets of a much later date. These
are covered with a pattern of gay tiled work, but
the workmanship is far inferior to the older portion of the structure. The whole of this splendid
building, both in color and design, is one of the
most striking examples of Mohammedan art to
be found in Persia.

Soon after our arrival, an official who appeared to hold a position similar to that of chief
of police called to request us to keep away from
the vicinity of the shrine. He followed all our
movements, explaining that the population of

Kum was in a state of religious excitement on account of the approaching anniversary of the saint, and that at such a time he felt responsible for our safety. We were, therefore, obliged to content ourselves with a distant view of the mosque, to be obtained from our windows in an upper story of the caravansary, nor were we permitted to approach even the outer gates during our stay.

The men of Kum pride themselves on a great reputation for piety, and show a corresponding intolerance towards all unbelievers. The streets are filled with the turbans of mollahs and seyids, in every shade of white, blue, and green. Even among the street beggars many wore the holy color that marked their claim to be kinsmen of the Prophet. During a visit to the bazars we were followed by a large crowd of idlers, curious to see European travellers, but except for the annoyance of being somewhat rudely jostled and pressed upon, we were not interfered with in any way. Here we made a number of additions to our outfit, replacing some of the bulky European " conveniences " we had brought with us from Constantinople, by more suitable articles such as are used by the Persians when on their travels; these included several thickly-wadded quilts, to be used either as covers or mattresses; heavy sheepskin coats, worn with the wool inside, the outer surface covered with elaborate embroidery, and native hoods to protect our heads and faces from the cold winds.

A large part of the bazar, like the town itself, is falling into ruin, although the passing caravans and pilgrims still bring with them considerable trade. The burial of the dead seems to be the one flourishing industry of Kum, and the whole town is now little else than a vast cemetery. Beyond the gates we were forced to pass through acres of neglected cenotaphs, that mark the last resting-places of pious Mohammedans whose bodies have been sent from miles around for burial within the sacred shadow of the golden dome. The bones of these belated pilgrims, packed in long boxes, and carried on the backs of pack-animals like so much merchandise, are a familiar sight of the caravan road. The relatives and friends of the deceased seldom accompany the remains, and appear to trust to the honesty of the mollahs of Kum to give them a decent burial, which is, of course, well paid for in advance. I was told that the Government now orders that bodies sent in this way must first have been buried for a certain length of time near the place of their decease. Until a few years ago, however, there was no such restriction, and the corpses for Kum and Kerbela travelled in hideous caravans whose approach could be traced for miles by the flocks of crows and carrion birds that hovered over the line of march. Messengers were sent ahead to warn the villagers along the way, and the peasants would close their houses and retire to a safe distance until the awful funeral procession had passed. Many of the camel-drivers who accompanied these convoys died on the way, and often pestilences were traced to this time-honored custom. At last the Government, to the great indignation of the priesthood, forbade this mode of transport.

At the present day in the case of some great personage, the rule as to local burial is occasionally relaxed, and the body travels in an elegant litter—as quickly as possible—to its destination, accompanied by sorrowing relatives and friends. The European traveller who has

NEAR KUM—A CORPSE CARAVAN

LOOKING FOR A NIGHT'S LODGING

been forced to pass a night in the same caravansary as one of these funeral parties, is not likely
to forget the experience, for several reasons.

At Kum we branched off from the main road
of travel which passes by Ispahan and Shiraz
to follow the old caravan track leading to Bagdad. Between Teheran and Kum a British company has built a carriage-road which is kept in a
passable state of repair. Traces of this enterprise are still to be found beyond Kum as far as
Sultanabad, but as four-wheeled vehicles are almost unknown, and except in bad weather there
is no especial reason to prevent a caravan from
taking a short cut across the open country, there
appears but little inducement for such private
enterprises as toll roads.

The portion of the British road which is still
under the company's control is by no means a
model of engineering, but beyond Kum, where
the highway is under the management of native
officials, it simply baffles description. Since the
pilgrimage of the late Shah to Kerbela, some
years ago, practically nothing has been done to
keep the caravan road in repair, and whatever
improvements may have been made at that time

have long since disappeared. After the winter rains the road becomes little more than a narrow slough, through which the horses flounder, sinking over their fetlocks in the sticky soil at every step. In many such places we found great walls of stone built at right angles to the track in order to prevent passing caravans from seeking a better path across the fields. The incredible shiftlessness and absolute lack of public spirit which characterizes most Eastern countries has left many useful monuments of the past to ruin and decay. Streams that we were forced to ford or else to cross by rickety wooden bridges we found still spanned by the remains of solidly-built brick bridges, paved with broad flat stones. Many of these lack only an arch or two—undermined by generations of flood and storm—to make them perfectly serviceable once more, but it is doubtful if the Persians to-day possess the necessary engineering skill to make these repairs, even had they the energy to do so. Ruins of many fine old caravansaries, substantially built of stone, proved the importance of the traffic which once must have passed along this old " Highway of the Nations." To-day these ruins are inhabited by bands of Persian nomads, who make themselves at home in the court-yards and porticos, to the exclusion of other travellers. This we found especially annoying when, as it often happened, we were forced to choose between sleeping in the open or sharing the populous interior of some native hut.

Our little cavalcade was an object of the liveliest curiosity to every band of merchants or pilgrims that we chanced to meet. First in our line of march came four slow-stepping pack-horses, loaded down with our valises and European camp outfit, besides a number of miscellaneous packages carried in the native khorjeens, or saddle-bags. On one of these loaded animals rode Meshedi Abbas, our personal servant. His dress was a long blue frock coat adorned with brass buttons, and he usually went armed with a rusty musket about five feet long, as a protection against the dangers of the way. At intervals throughout the day, Abbas falling asleep, the unbalanced load would topple off, depositing him and his weapon with a crash on the stony road, and as he often forgot to remove the percussion caps, I was kept in daily anticipation of a tragedy that would wipe out our entire company at one fell blow.

Our other retainers were a charvadar, or mule-driver, and a decrepit old man who was supposed to be part owner of the horses that made up the caravan. The former was a cheery, stupid giant, dressed in the coarse blue canvas worn by the Persian peasantry, while old Hadji affected the dingy flowing robe of a Persian townsman. On several occasions we tried in vain to leave this venerable nuisance behind, as his constant complaining wore sadly on the nerves of every one. But although he rode a deformed and half-blind horse, he managed to keep abreast with the others by some process of his own (I had my suspicions of a needle, but was never able to catch him at it). Besides our regular attendants, a number of stragglers usually managed to attach themselves to the caravan on one excuse or another. At one time we were accompanied for some distance by a veritable beggar on horseback, who could not understand our indignant refusal to give him alms. On another occasion we were joined by a picturesque young darvish, carrying an axe and a begging-bowl, whom

Abbas described as a "Very Holy Boy." He was, indeed, quite an addition to our party, for in spite of his sacred character he made himself generally useful with the horses, in return for our protection and a modest share of the evening meal.

Distances in Persia are measured by "farsakhs," a variable measure supposed to be the distance travelled by a laden mule during a given time. Five or six of these stages are supposed to constitute a day's journey, but we learned to put very little confidence in the reports we found set down in the books of previous travellers. During the winter months, when it is impossible to use the ruined caravansaries travellers along the Bagdad trail are forced to seek such hospitality as the native huts afford. By far the worst trial we had to bear during the journey was the nightly contact at close quarters with the native life. After a long day's ride in the crisp open air, to come into the stifling atmosphere of a Persian khané, reeking with the odors of Oriental housekeeping, then to have our tired limbs assailed throughout the night by an army of relentless insect pests, was at times almost unbearable. For a long while it was a mystery to me how the natives could support the plague they bring upon themselves by their filthy and negligent habits, but after some weeks it became apparent to us that by a process of inoculation or tanning one becomes immune to a certain extent against the attacks of all but the most venomous species. When we had the good fortune to pass the night in a caravansary, we invariably chose the most dilapidated and deserted quarters to be found, in preference to the guests' room used by Persian travellers. Even then, from every nook and cranny the heat would bring forth legions of tormentors, who had probably been lying dormant since the days of Shah Abbas, and fell upon us with appetites whetted by their long fast.

I dwell on this rather unpleasant subject at some length, because I have frequently been asked if there is any reason why " tourists," or ladies, should not enjoy the pleasures of travelling in Persia, and moreover, because I have never found a book of travel, however eloquent, which in any way does justice to this feature of life in the " Golden East."

A PERSIAN CARAVAN

The day after leaving Kum we pressed forward under a hot sun for four farsakhs to Rygiert, a large village at the foot of the trail leading into the mountains. The condition of the road was such that we arrived at Rygiert some time after nightfall, and were forced to put up with the only lodgings we could find, in the stable of a half-ruined caravansary. To add to our discomfort, we found that the cave-like room we were to occupy had lost the heavy wooden shutter which usually closes the single opening that serves at the same time as door and window. A glance at the group around a little fire near the entrance gate had shown me that our fellow-lodgers belonged to the lowest class of travellers on the caravan road, so that I was by no means pleased with the prospect of sleeping thus unprotected in their vicinity. Making the best of the situation, however, we barricaded the doorway with all the heavy baggage in our possession, and improvised besides a rude burglar-alarm with a tin kettle propped on a couple of sticks. In the middle of the night we were awakened by the clatter of its fall, and the sound of running feet in the distance told us that our

precaution had not been in vain. The sequel
to this episode was most amusing and threw an
interesting light on the manners and customs of
Persian rogues.

For not content with attempting to rob us,
one of our ingenious fellow-lodgers had the
audacity to charge our muleteer with having
stolen a pistol and a sum of money from the
saddle-bags of one of his pack-animals. The
fellow, who claimed to be a camel-driver in the
service of the Grand Vizir, even insisted that our
" charvadar " should return to Kum and swear
his innocence of the theft at Fatmah's Shrine,
a form of trial greatly in favor among the
Persians. The idea appeared to me so ludicrous
that at first I was inclined to doubt his sincerity,
but when we threatened to proceed on our
journey, he summoned his friends and a mob of
villagers to bar our progress. Things were taking on a serious aspect when our servant Abbas
proposed a solution of this knotty theological
problem which appeared to satisfy all parties
concerned. Our muleteer agreed to take seven
steps in the direction of the Holy City, and then,
raising his hands, to swear that he actually stood

in the midst of the Sacred Shrine. A small pile
of stones was then raised near the roadside to
take the place of the catafalque that marks the
last resting-place of Imam Reza's sister, and
these curious rites having been performed to the
satisfaction of all concerned, the innocence of the
supposed culprit appeared to be established, and
we all parted on the best of terms.

(*January 22*) Soon after leaving the village
of Dowletabad we had an adventure which
showed us that bad as the caravan track may be,
it is often dangerous to abandon its ruts and pitfalls and strike across country on an independent
route. A few miles beyond the village we attempted to take a short cut across a salt marsh,
following the muddy track of a caravan which
had preceded us but a short time before. As
luck would have it, however, we had progressed
but a few miles when we were overtaken by a
violent snow-storm, accompanied by a furious
wind that drove the blinding flakes straight in
our faces. Soon the bunches of salt grass which
grew on either side of the track, marking the
way, became invisible, and our pack-animals began to wander from the road and to flounder in

the stiff frozen mud of the marsh. Our situation was an unpleasant one, for our tracks had now disappeared so that we found it as dangerous to go back as to proceed. However, luck was in our favor, and just as we were preparing to camp in the snow, inevitably risking frost-bites, the warm Persian sun broke through the clouds, and we saw but a short distance before us the mud walls of the caravansary of Harounabad, where we spent the night in relative comfort.

(*January 26*) Our little caravan is now approaching Kermanshah, the ancient capital of Persian Kurdistan. From a broad plain before us, checkered with little green fields of irrigated land, rises the famous Rock of Bisitun, a great natural monument that marks the beginning of the trail through the passes of the Zagros Mountains which has been the principal highway of war and commerce between the Iranian plateau and the plains of Mesopotamia since the dawn of history. This great crag, the last of a range of small jagged peaks that stretch out from the high mountains beyond, is shaped like a huge pyramid with one of its faces rising almost vertical from the plain. The Persians attribute its peculiar form to the prodigious labors of the sculptor Ferhad, one of several marvellous feats he performed for love of the beautiful Shireen, wife of Khosros the Magnificent. But on the mountain's face are sculptured records that were already old when the real Shireen dwelt, a young princess, in the halls of her father, the Greek emperor Maurice. Carved deep in the imperishable rock, Darius Hystaspes, returning from the conquest of the lowlands to his Persian capital, has left a record of his greatness. The spot chosen by Darius for his famous inscriptions is the south wall of a deep cleft running down the sheer face of the rock. Just below lies a broad pool that sends a cold little river bubbling across the plain, while near by among the tombstones of a modern Kurdish cemetery stand the broken columns of a Greek temple. We had some difficulty in procuring guides to take us to this spot, as nightfall was approaching and the Kurdish villagers declared the place to be haunted by the spirits of the dead.

The entrance to the cleft or opening I have spoken of is indeed an eerie spot. As we drew near the rocky walls sent back strange echoes, like the complaining of a great voice. High above our heads towered the sheer battlements of the rock of Bisitun, every peak aflame in the sunset glow. Across the face of the cliff a pair of Persian eagles swept proudly back and forth with outstretched wings, the only living creatures in sight. On either side of the stony track we were following the trees and bushes were covered with white rags and strips of gay-colored cloth, tied to the branches by pious pilgrims as offerings to the spirit guardians of the place.

The inscriptions and the group of statues we had come to see are carved high on the sheer face of the cliff. They represent Darius and seven captive kings who are led in judgment before him. Over the head of the Persian Emperor hovers the winged crest of Ahura Mazda, while each king is labelled with his name and titles. Seen from below, their size appeared insignificant, but when one of our Kurdish guides by dint of digging his bare toes into the invisible crevices of a pathway known only to the initiated, succeeded in reaching a stone platform just below them, I saw that the figures we had judged to be but some three feet in height are, as a

matter of fact, of heroic size. Near these interesting bas-reliefs is carved a long inscription in
ancient Persian, Median, and Assyrian, recount-
ing Darius' glorious adventures and setting forth
his royal titles.

To the archæologist these inscriptions of
Bisitun are of peculiar interest. It was here
that the English *savant* Rawlinson first discov-
. ered the key to the cuneiform characters of the
Babylonian inscriptions, which enabled him to
decipher the countless records of Assyrian do-
minion scattered all through the plains of
Mesopotamia.

Following the example of Darius, other
Persian monarchs and conquerors have recorded
their deeds on the imperishable rock. A little
beyond the famous bas-relief of Darius, the
whole face of the cliff has been prepared to
receive a monument or inscription on a still
grander scale. The surface shows everywhere
tool-marks like those of a gigantic chisel, while
the plain below is strewn with huge blocks of
stone, torn from the face of the cliff, evidently
quarried by means of some cyclopean machine.
It would be difficult, even with our perfect en-

gineering appliances, to duplicate the work of
the engineers and artists who carved their names
for all eternity on the face of Bisitun, and I
cannot but think there is some truth in the
theories lately advanced by a French scientist,
who holds that these ancient builders had at their
command a knowledge of the principles of me-
chanics unknown to us to-day. Until this question be authoritatively settled, I have heard no
explanation so satisfactory as that offered by the
simple inhabitants of the Kurdish villages in the
neighborhood, who attribute these marvellous
remains to the handiwork of the genii, who they
believe still make their homes among the crags
and peaks of Bisitun.

During the night following our visit to the
Rock of Bisitun, a heavy fall of snow closed the
mountain passes on the way to Kermanshah,
making the trail impracticable until some passing
camel caravan should trample a way through the
deep snow. We were, therefore, obliged to wait
patiently in our rude quarters in a Kurdish village whose name I was unable to ascertain.
Here we spent the day, imprisoned between the
four mud walls of a windowless room, cowering

over a smoky fire and battling with the insect population that swarmed out from every crack and cranny to make us welcome. The visits of curious villagers and the doings of our host's family in the dirty court-yard below were our only distractions, and needless to say time hung heavily on our hands.

These Persian Kurds are a handsome race, and appear fairly happy in spite of their miserable surroundings. The winter costume of the men consists of a long overcoat of gray felt worn over a short embroidered jacket, to which bright rows of brass rifle-cartridges are often sewn by way of ornament. The rest of the costume is made up of baggy trousers of the ordinary Turkish cut, descending to the ankles, and boots or slippers of soft leather. The women, like the Persian peasant women, go about unveiled. They wear short jackets that leave the throat and chest bare, and voluminous skirts of Turkey-red cotton cloth. Even the poorest wear a profusion of ornaments, such as glass beads, anklets, and bracelets made from strings of coins. The old women are pitiful creatures, worn and bent by toil and privation, but many of

the younger girls are strikingly pretty. Their
principal accomplishment is dancing, and some
of the native steps, performed to the groaning
accompaniment of a weird chant, are decidedly
interesting if not graceful. Probably the beauties of Kurdish dancing, like the finer points of
Kurdish music, will never appeal to the uniniti-
ated taste of the Occidental mind. Indeed, the
latter appeared to me more like the groaning of
a person in agony than the expression of more
pleasing sentiments.

Next morning we found the snow rapidly
melting in the warm air of a bright sunny day.
The trail was already trodden into a deep morass
by the feet of passing caravans, and our poor
horses sank above their fetlocks at every step.
We had gone but a mile or so when my little
gray slipped and fell on his side, pinning me
beneath him. Fortunately the roadbed was so
soft that I was unhurt, but covered with
mud from head to foot for my entry into
Kermanshah.

From a distance this important town, the
ancient capital of Persian Kurdistan, presents
quite an imposing appearance, but nearer ap-

AMONG THE KURDS—DANCING GIRLS

proach ends, as usual, in disillusion. Once within
its walls, we found some difficulty in making our
way through the narrow winding streets, our
horses plunging and stumbling over the piles of
snow and frozen mud, which encumbered the
roadway, every instant threatening to dash out
our brains against the walls of the houses on
either side. After threading this maze for some
time, keeping a careful watch meanwhile to see
that none of our horses should stray off or be
driven into the open doorways of the houses
on either side, we came at last to the house of
the Vakil-ed-Dowleh, the native British Agent,
to whom we had letters from our friends at the
English Legation at Teheran.

Like most of the houses of Kermanshah, the
exterior of the Vakil's residence was anything
but imposing, but within it was furnished with
a degree of Oriental comfort we had not seen
since we left Teheran. Our host received us,
seated cross-legged on a handsome rug before a
low table covered with writing material, in a long
room opening on an inner court-yard where a
tiled fountain was playing in the sunshine.
After we had exchanged greetings, a servant

brought fine gilded chairs for us, and another presented us with a water-pipe or kalian, after first puffing at it vigorously himself to set the yellow tobacco burning. The Vakil speaks no English, so our interview was confined to the few very general remarks I was able to make in Persian. After a few moments of this Ollendorfian conversation, we were conducted to our rooms. These we found crowded with chairs and tables of European manufacture, but the beds on which we longed to stretch our weary limbs were conspicuous by their absence, beds being an almost unknown luxury in Persia. Seeing our dilemma a great pile of cushions were brought, and on these we passed a comfortable night, the first spent beneath a friendly roof since we had left Sultanabad.

The next morning, after an ample breakfast of jellied eggs, rose-leaf preserves, and great golden rolls of Persian bread, we started out with our host to visit the Governor of Kermanshah. We were accompanied through the narrow streets by a couple of footmen armed with heavy maces to clear the throngs of beggars from our path, and followed by a dozen or more

of the Vakil's friends and retainers, so that our
party presented an imposing appearance. The
Governor's Palace is a large building, standing
in the midst of a garden laid out in the best
Persian style, the trees growing in long formal
rows, with many tiled fountains playing in their
midst. We found his Excellency awaiting us,
with his son and a young Mohammedan priest
who had been educated in India and spoke excellent English. Like all Persians he asked us
many questions about our intentions in visiting
his country, and what impression it had made
upon us. He was filled with respect at the sight
of a small photograph I had taken of his Imperial master the Shah, in Teheran, and pressed
it reverently to his lips and forehead. His satisfaction, moreover, was great when I took his own
portrait and he urged me to send him a copy as
soon as possible. After our visit to the Governor
we paid our respects to the High Priest, who
lives in a small house near the principal mosque
of the city. This important personage we found
to be a little old man whose huge white turban
and great horn spectacles gave him a very
learned and reverent bearing. His scanty beard,

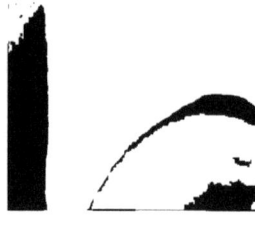

a Cossack sergeant of Persian extraction, who acted as guide. They seemed anxious to impress us with the fact that they were travelling for pleasure alone, and in return appeared very curious as to our motives for visiting Persia. One of them, a rather pompous young man with a long yellow beard, was especially persistent in this respect. He wore a brilliant Circassian uniform or costume, which made a tremendous impression on the native population, and had evidently been instructed to do things handsomely, as his generosity to the servants of the Vakil and the beggars of the town was as lavish as it was ostentatious. After dinner, having absorbed a good deal more of our host's Persian wine than was good for him, he commenced in a very patronizing manner to warn me against the dangers of the way before us, leaving me to infer that it was only their prestige as Russian officers which had enabled them to come through in safety. Readily divining his object, I favored him in return with an account of our journey to Kermanshah, which left him in a state of alcoholic panic, for his credulity was apparently only equalled by his belief in his own powers of dissimulation.

I afterwards had an agreeable conversation with his companion, Col. S——, who talked in a very interesting way about their journey. It is a highly significant fact that a great part of their route lay across a country which at that time was supposed to be absolutely closed to Europeans. It is also certain that similar parties of Russian explorers, with the main object of getting into friendly relations with the native population, are travelling in the most inaccessible and out-of-the-way parts of Persia and Central Asia, and the Russian uniform is a not unfamiliar sight in many " unexplored " corners of the Middle East.

VIII.

NEAR the vague frontier that separates Persian Kurdistan from the Turkish provinces in Mesopotamia, lies the little border town of Kasr-Shahrin. On the crest of a steep hill rising abruptly from a well-watered plain, one sees from afar its small brick fortress, with the flat-roofed mud dwellings of a large Kurdish village clustering about its base. This stronghold is the residence of a Persian Governor, who, at the head of some two thousand Kurdish riflemen, holds the border in true feudal style.

While their fellow-tribesmen, just across the border in Turkish territory, enjoy a reputation for unrestrained lawlessness which makes them the terror of their more peaceful Persian neighbors, on the principle of " setting a thief to catch a thief " the Kurdish population of Kasr-Shahrin forms one of the finest regiments of irregular cavalry to be found in the Persian army, and the pious pilgrims on the great high road to Kerbela travel their way in peace under the safe guard of these unnatural protectors.

As we rode up the steep road that leads to the Governor's Palace I was impressed, as often before in this out-of-the-way corner of the world, with the medieval character of the picturesque scene before us. Men-at-arms in flowing robes were busy polishing their weapons, or lounged about in the sunshine before the doorway. A hawker surrounded by an interested group was giving the first lesson to a newly-caught eyas, letting the bird fly for a short distance, then gently pulling it back towards him by a long string fastened to its leg. A ragged darvish with his begging-bowl passed among these loiterers, shouting an insolent demand for alms, while on a broad flight of steps leading to an arched portico sat a group of peasants patiently waiting their turn to be received in audience by the great man above, each one bringing with him some little tribute of country produce— a basket of ripe melons, or a brace of gaunt Persian fowls.

After a long parley at the door, we were admitted to the presence of his Excellency, whom we found in an upper room seated on a low divan near a window that commanded a magnificent view of the green valley below and the snow-clad Zagros Mountains in the distance. Behind the Governor, on the same divan, sat his secretary, cross-legged, writing at a little table raised a few inches from the ground, while along the wall opposite a number of grave-looking Kurds squatted on their heels in the knee-breaking attitude which Orientals assume, apparently with comfort, for hours at a time.

His Excellency addressed us through the medium of his secretary, who spoke French with some fluency, asking us innumerable questions as to our destination, why we had come, etc.; for travellers in Persian Kurdistan are still rare enough to be objects of official suspicion. However, our letters of introduction from Teheran appeared to reassure him, and he ended by urging us to spend some time at Kasr-Shahrin, promising us that good sport of all kinds was to be enjoyed in the neighborhood. Indeed, if we were to believe his account, the plains about the town fairly swarmed with antelope and small game, while in the mountains near by were to be found leopards, moufflons (or mountain sheep), and wild asses—this latter, the fabulous

" onager " of early Oriental travellers, looked
upon by the Persians as the wildest and rarest of
their native game.

Our interview ended, lodgings were procured for us in a house near the fortress by the
simple process of forcing the reluctant owner, a
wealthy Kurd, to move out during our stay.
Scarcely had we installed ourselves, when as a
fresh proof of the Governor's good will there
arrived great platters filled with fruit and native
cheese, together with baked meats and half of a
freshly-killed antelope. For these offerings we
had to pay a cash present to our host's servants,
as Persian etiquette demands that an immediate
return shall be made for all such courtesies. It
will be seen that the far-famed Oriental hospitality is somewhat different from that in vogue in
the Occident.

The household arrangements of a Kurdish
chieftain are primitive enough to satisfy the most
ardent followers of the " Simple Life." The
house so summarily placed at our disposal con-
sisted of but two stories, the lower containing
the stables, where the men servants slept among
the sheep and horses; the upper divided into two

apartments, the selamlik for the male members of
the family, and the anderoun, inhabited by the
women and children. The roughly plastered
walls were pierced by deep niches, which serve to
hold such household effects as are not in constant
use. The hard earthen floor was covered with a
thick felt carpet, and over this were spread the
fine Kurdish rugs which serve as seats by day and
couches by night.

In the middle of the floor a fire-blackened
hole about two feet in diameter marked the spot
where in winter the " courcy " is set over a pot
of burning charcoal. This primitive but very
effective heating apparatus consists of a frame-
work of wood some two feet high and five feet
square, over which are spread heavy coverings
to retain the heat of the fire beneath. During
the long winter months the Persian and Kurdish
peasants spend their time cowering beneath these
shelters, with only their heads and shoulders exposed to the outer air. We soon found this
native fashion the only effective way of keeping
warm in cold weather, as the construction of the
average Kurdish house is better adapted to ven-
tilation than warmth.

The sandy deserts and barren mountain-slopes of Western Persia are the hunting-ground of all kinds of feathered freebooters. Here are found the great eagles of the Kurdish hills, long- and short-winged hawks of every variety, and in-numerable species of sparrow-hawks and smaller birds of prey. These broad reaches of earth and sky are the true home of Falconry; from time immemorial man must have sought to turn to his own profit the matchless instinct of these winged hunters, and centuries before the art of hawking became known in Europe it was per-fected on the plains of Kurdistan and Mesopo-tamia. From these Eastern lands some chance traveller or returned crusader brought its secrets and traditions to become the " delighte of chiv-allrie " during three centuries among the woods and fields of Europe.

The art of Falconry, once so popular in Europe that every lord and gentleman counted among his retinue of servants a train of skilled falconers, is to-day almost as obsolete in Europe as the tilting-yard and the forgotten pastimes we read of in the pages of the Knightly Chronicles. The sport which once delighted

MESHEDI ABBAS

OUR RETAINERS

HAWKING NEAR KERMANSHAH

our English ancestors is practically unknown in America, and even in England at the present time the few establishments that are still kept up depend rather on the antiquarian tastes of their owners than on any real usefulness in the field. In the Orient, however, in common with most travellers who have ventured from the more beaten tracks, I have frequently had occasion to witness the spectacle of the " mid-air chase," and in the following pages I propose to describe this ancient and poetic sport as it is practised to-day in all the countries of the East, where civilization has not taught the native to prefer the slaughter of game by mechanical means to the finer sensations of the old arts of Vénerie.

Early the day after our arrival in Kasr-Shahrin, a messenger came from the Governor, inviting us to join a hunting party to be given that afternoon in honor of some visiting Kurdish chieftains. At the appointed hour we saw a picturesque cavalcade issue from the gateway of the fortress and wind its way down the steep pathway leading to the town. Riding first came a party of Kurdish soldiers, a wild-looking lot, armed with repeating rifles, rows of bright brass cartridges, sewn to their short wadded jackets, giving them the appearance of being dressed in armor. Behind this rather suspicious-looking escort against the dangers of the way rode a party of the Governor's guests and their retainers, most of them dressed in the Kurdish national costume, baggy white breeches, short blue jackets, covered with rich embroidery, with long flowing white sleeves, trailing almost to the ground as they rode. All were mounted on powerful little Arab horses, covered from mane to crupper with gay-colored saddle-cloths, the finest product of the native looms. With the exception of a few servants, every man carried on his right wrist his favorite hawk, the fierce little brown birds, blinded by their leather hoods, quietly awaiting their share in the day's proceedings.

In the midst of this picturesque company appeared our host, the Governor, wearing a blue uniform with large gold epaulets. A long visored jockey cap of gray cloth and a large pair of black goggles gave the finishing touches to a costume doubtless intended to impress us with his knowledge of the latest European fashions.

By his side rode his Chief Hawker, an old man with a gray beard dyed a flaming scarlet with henna juice. Around his felt cap was wound a dingy turban of green cloth, to show that he was a seyid, or descendant of the Prophet, which even in his menial capacity earned for him a certain consideration; while the lowering glances he cast from time to time in our direction proved his peculiar sanctity and pious hatred of the unbeliever. Indeed, so sinister was the aspect of this old fanatic that I secretly resolved not to trust myself to his guidance farther than necessity might demand.

At the Governor's left rode an attendant whose duty it was to keep ever ready for his master the ubiquitous kalian, or Persian water-pipe. To properly prepare this cumbersome instrument for use is no light task, even under the most favorable conditions, while to keep the red-hot coals freshly burning over the coarse tobacco when mounted on a rapidly-moving horse would appear a difficult feat. A pot of live charcoal swung from the saddle-bow, and from this the kalian-bearer dexterously renewed his tinder each time the Governor called for a fresh pipe, puffing vigorously at the long stem himself meanwhile, to keep it ever ready to pass to his master. Bringing up the rear of the procession, came a long train of pack-animals gay with worsted trappings and clanging bells, bearing great hampers of provisions and a small tent in case the Governor should be disposed to take a siesta by the way.

As we rode through the narrow streets of the old Kurdish town it required some caution to keep our horses from falling among the deep pits and quagmires of soft mud that marked the way, even in the principal thoroughfares. After a further scramble across the mounds and falling gravestones of an old Mohammedan graveyard, we found ourselves in the open country among the fields and well-watered gardens that lie along the banks of the river. The country about Kasr-Shahrin must at one time have supported a large and flourishing population. Scattered everywhere about the neighborhood are mounds and artificial elevations that mark the sites of buried towns and palaces. It frequently happens that among the rude coins current in the outlying villages one comes upon some beautiful Greek

OUR HOST AND HIS FAVORITE HAWKS

HAWKING—A KILL.

specimens of the Seleucian period, still currently used as money by the peasants.

Not far from the modern town lie the remains of a great city and palace built by Khosros the Magnificent. Persian tradition has it that these cyclopean remains are the result of the labors of the hero Ferhad—the Oriental Hercules —whose love for the wife of Khosros, the beauteous Shireen, is a favorite theme of the Persian poets. For some time we skirted the massive wall built by this matchless lover from giant blocks of roughly-hewn stone, to-day covered with vines and parasitic plants, then, entering by a wide breach, perhaps the very opening forced by the victorious Greeks, we found ourselves in the midst of Khosros' citadel. Before us lay the ruins of a group of gigantic buildings, the palaces and temples of the Persian monarch, while the wall itself enclosed a space many acres in extent once covered by the mud-brick houses of his dependants and the gardens and pleasure-grounds of the " Great King." Aside from the legend of Ferhad and his mythical labors, there must, indeed, have been " Giants in those days." The walls and arches still standing are built of small blocks of roughly-hewn stone, but lying all about are fallen lintels and monolith to handle which would test the skill of our modern engineers and their most perfected appliances. The knowledge of masonry and the bold constructions of the vaulting shown in several of the buildings that still defy the ravages of time, is truly remarkable. In one structure the roof is carried on diagonal pointed arches thrown across the corners of a square plan, an artifice that would have done credit to the monkish builders who reared the cathedrals of Medieval Europe. But now:—

> " The lion and the lizard keep
> The courts where Jamshid gloried and drank deep.
> And Bahram, that great Hunter—the Wild Ass
> Stamps o'er his head, but cannot break his sleep."

Among the empty halls and chambers of the magnificent Khosros' pleasure-house lay the field of our afternoon's sport. For the thickets of camel-thorn growing everywhere among the ruined palaces now give cover to great flocks of partridges and bustards, while on the river's brink, where Shireen and her maids may oft have descended the marble steps to bathe in the crystal stream, grow thick beds of reed where the water-fowl build their nests.

A pack of feathery-eared Persian grey-hounds, and a brace of mongrel setters brought from Europe of which our host was exceedingly proud, ranged far and near through the little plantations of grain and vegetables which lay in every favorable hollow among the ruined walls. Suddenly from one of these patches of culti-vated ground a couple of birds rose from under the noses of the dogs, and winged their way up a stony ravine. From all sides sounded the cry of " Kap! " " Kap! " (the Persian name for a species of grouse), and spurring on our horses re-gardless of the pitfalls in the shape of crumbling walls and gulleys filled with loose stones, we all clattered after at full speed. I could not but admire the horsemanship of the hawkers, who, with a dexterous movement unhooded their flut-tering charges and, poising themselves in the saddle, launched them in pursuit of the quarry, the operation being performed with the horse running at top speed.

Swift as were the whirring grouse in their flight, swifter still came the swoop of the unhooded hawk! The chase was but a short one; ending with a flash of white feathers as the stricken bird turned in the air. We came up just in time to see old " Red-Beard " luring the fierce little hunter from its quarry with a piece of fresh meat. I noticed that before pocketing the game the hawker carefully cut its throat, that blood might flow, according to the requirements of Mohammedan ritual. Had this important ceremony not been performed, the game would have been considered " unclean " and not fit to be eaten by a True Believer.

Leaving the scene of our first " kill," the whole cavalcade rode up the steep hill-side, following a narrow track made by flocks of sheep on their way to pasture in the higher valleys. Soon all about us grouse were taking wing, not rising as they do under ordinary circumstances, but flying close to the ground, ready to take refuge behind the nearest cover from the pursuing hawk. These, with their single fierce note, came swooping after, their silent graceful movements contrasting with the loud whirring flight of their prey. It was breakneck work to follow across the loose stones and bowlders that covered the hill-side. Often we were floundering across ditches and gullies, the snow, up to our horses' girths hiding all kinds of pitfalls and dangers, now headed towards the white peaks above, now slipping and sliding down towards the valley below.

My Persian gray soon began to show that this kind of work was little to his taste, for his long legs betokened the plainsman, and I often envied my companions their sturdy little mountain horses as I flogged along far in their rear. At last I found I had lost my companions altogether. Once or twice in the far distance I saw a horseman silhouetted against the sky; then these disappeared, and I found myself alone on the Kurdish hill-side, the noise of the chase growing fainter and fainter in the distance.

My position at best was an unpleasant one, for I had no idea in which direction to turn, and to ask my way was quite out of the question. Even should I meet with any of the wild herders who inhabit these hills, it would have been the height of folly to trust myself to their guidance. Presently, however, to my great relief, I caught sight of my host's faithful kalian-bearer pounding along below me, with his various utensils rattling like a tin-shop in an earthquake. Knowing that sooner or later he would become the center of interest, I spurred my jaded horse down to meet him, and soon, one by one, the tired huntsmen put in their appearance, some with two or three tawny bunches of feathers hanging from their saddle, others without even their hawks to show for their afternoon's work.

Then followed the long ride homeward through the gathering twilight, while the setting sun drew the light and color from the world into one band of flaming crimson along the Western horizon. Against the evening sky rose the mysterious fastnesses and untrodden peaks of the Kurdish hills, aflame in the ruddy glow, while in the darkening foreground lay the little oasis of Kasr-Shahrin with its high-walled gardens of palm trees and checkered fields of corn and grain. Overhead the radiant southern stars came out, one by one, like bright lamps hanging low over the bare winter desert, and the mystery of the empty world about us threw a spell of silence on the wild horsemen of our cavalcade. Forward into the night we rode without a sound except the trampling hoof-beats, or when some weary hawk, raising its drooping wings, would utter a long high scream of protest against its blind captivity.

The short day's march that separates Kasr-Shahrin from the Turkish border town of Khanekin is looked upon by the pilgrims who travel the Bagdad trail as the most dangerous part of their journey. For this reason they usually travel from the former place in large companies and heavily armed. This is on account of the " No-man's-land " along the frontier that divides Persia from the Ottoman Empire, which is often infested by bands of outlaws and ruffians who profit by the ready opportunity of taking refuge across either border to commit all sorts of outrages, sometimes in Persian and sometimes in Turkish territory.

Our little party on the march presented a very determined front; all the weapons we were able to muster were conspicuously displayed and kept in readiness for instant use. Every passing traveller was an object of suspicion, and every rock and hill capable of concealing an enemy was carefully reconnoitred by the vigilant Abbas.

I do not know whether the dangers he represented existed only in the vivid imagination of our friends at Kasr-Shahrin, but at any rate we met with no adventures until we found ourselves well within Turkish territory.

The Turkish frontier is guarded by a chain of brick towers or fortresses, each one garrisoned by a handful of zaptiehs. We also passed at intervals patrols of Turkish cavalrymen whose duty is to prevent smuggling and to keep Persian pilgrims from slipping across the border without paying the tax that the Turkish Government levies on all visitors to the Sultan's dominions. We found Khanekin to be quite a busy little town, surrounded by beautiful groves of palm trees. Here we were entertained by an Armenian doctor in charge of the new Turkish quarantine, who, strange to relate, had been educated in New York, and had travelled besides over the greater part of the United States. In exchange for his hospitality we told the news of Manhattan to this far exile on the borders of the Mesopotamian desert, and I cannot but believe his many assurances that our visit was a welcome one.

Beyond the borders of Persia the fertile rol-
ing country of the Zagros foothills slopes away
to meet the level floor of the great Mesopotamian desert. The plains covered with short grass
through which we had been travelling gave way
to broad stretches of golden sand. Here the only
traces of vegetation to be seen are occasional
patches of yellow reeds and brown withered
grasses. The caravan track becomes a broad,
trampled highway, scarcely to be distinguished
from the surrounding plain except for the skele-
tons of camels and other pack-animals that have
fallen by the road-side.

A couple of stages beyond Khanekin we
learned that it would be possible to take an
" araba " or native wagon and push on without
further delay to Bagdad. Leaving our caravan
to follow at its own slow pace, we would thus
gain three days at least on our journey. After
three weeks spent in the saddle we were not long
in making up our minds to embrace this unexpected opportunity of escaping from the monotony of desert travel.

We set out at midnight, taking only Abbas
and leaving Hadji and the muleteers in charge

of the pack-animals. An "araba" we found to be a springless wagon, on the bottom of which we reclined at length on a thin mattress stuffed with straw. We were drawn swiftly across the level of the desert by four little mules driven by a Bedouin in a red garment like a night-shirt, with a boy assistant who flogged the backs of our long-eared steeds continuously and impartially with a heavy whip. While riding horseback I would have sworn that nothing came nearer realizing the definition of a plane surface than the level floor of the Mesopotamian desert, but our rough vehicle rolled and tossed like a ship at sea, every now and again crashing in and out of deep irrigating ditches with a shock that would have reduced any ordinary conveyance to kindling-wood. On the way Abbas tried to beguile us with further tales of "bad Arabs," who were supposed to infest these roads, and indeed the horsemen we passed, armed with spears and rifles, their faces muffled in Bedouin hoods, had anything but a reassuring appearance.

Sunrise found us travelling across a level plain of sand stretching unbroken on every side of us as far as the eye could reach—the true desert as I had always pictured it: "The abode of emptiness," indeed! As the sun climbed towards the zenith and the fantastic shadows of our equipages grew short on the sands, a wind from the heated leagues that lay between us and Syria blew its burning breath in our faces. Like mariners lost on some Sargasson sea, we strained our eyes toward the horizon, hoping to catch the first sign that might tell us we were approaching the ancient city, the goal of so many weary marches.

The refraction of the sun's rays began to play familiar tricks; great lakes appeared before us, fading into pools of pearly mist as we approached. Distant caravans came into sight, each camel apparently elongated like some giant exclamation point, seeming to hang between earth and sky. The glare reflected from the white sands became almost insupportable. Our driver and his assistant dozed on their narrow perch, and our gallant team drooped their long ears dejectedly as they toiled forward under the vertical beams. Every living creature except the desert crows, and ourselves, seemed to have taken refuge from the triumphant rays, and I began to appreciate the plight of the poor Arab who bought his horse from the Hoja but forgot to buy its shadow.

Then, suddenly, as we travelled listlessly forward across an empty world of sky and plain, a stroke of desert enchantment rent the veil of mist that hung along the pale horizon, and in the far distance we saw amidst the dark silhouette of feathery palm groves the gleaming domes and minarets of a dream city—Bagdad, the Capital of the Califs, lay before us at last!

IX.

THE house we occupied during our stay in Bagdad stood on the banks of the Tigris, so close to the swift muddy stream that from my balcony I might have dropped a pebble on the decks of some of the quaint river craft passing below. The animated scene I looked out upon was the same that delighted Sindbad when he returned from his voyages to inhabit his palace in the Capital of the Califs. Scarcely a spar or sail of the vessels which enlivened the broad surface of the river has changed since his day: graceful lateen-rigged " buggalows " with hulls of polished palm wood, sharp-prowed " golams " sculled along against the swift current by a long oar fixed at the stern, and—strangest of all—the Arab " goufas " of tarred skin stretched on a circular frame of basket work, the very boats seen on the stone carvings of Babylon and Nineveh. I was always reminded on seeing a party of Arabs in one of these strange craft of the story of the " Three wise men of Gotham who went to sea in a bowl," but they have, at any rate, the advantage claimed for them by the native boatmen, of always being headed in the right direction, no mean factor in navigating the swift current of the Tigris among its many shallows and sand-bars.

Modern Bagdad is built along both banks of the Tigris at a point where the fickle stream broadens for a space to a width of about a quarter of a mile. Long bridges of boats join the two portions of the town, the most important quarters lying on the right bank of the river. Bagdad has to-day shrunken to a fraction of its former size, but the ruins of the ancient suburbs, stretching for a long distance on both sides of the river among the palm groves of the Arab peasants, show that it must have been a very large city in ancient times, judged even by the standards of the present day.

From a high terrace before our house I looked out across a wide expanse of flat roofs on a panorama which has few equals in the Orient. Along the horizon the countless domes and minarets that mark the shrines of Mohammedan Saints and Holy Men lifted their graceful sil-

BAGDAD—STRANGE RIVER CRAFT ON THE TIGRIS

houettes against the eternal blue of the Eastern
sky: the dazzling white cupola of Abd-el-Kader's
shrine, the holiest in Bagdad, flanked by minarets
of turquoise blue; the high red brick tower, all
that remains of the splendid monument built by
Harun-el-Reshid over the grave of the fair
Zobeida; the great new dome of Daoud Pasha's
mosque covered with black and green tile-work,
decorated with bands of Arabic inscriptions; and
in the foreground along the river bank, white
palaces and villas that gleamed among the dark
foliaged orange- and lemon-trees, with terraces
and gardens descending to the water's edge.

From a distance it is still easy to imagine
Bagdad filled with the many splendors that the
old Arabian chronicles love to dwell upon.   But,
alas! on nearer approach most of these enchant-
ments fade away.   Our first walk through its
narrow streets showed us that the greater part of
the once-glorious City of Califs is given over to
ruin and decay, and in place of the fairy palaces
and marble halls of Harun's capital stand whitewashed walls of clay-brick or tottering ruins of
the past.

And this process of disintegration still goes

PUBLIC SQUARE IN BAGDAD

vilayet. Here, too, are found the principal
bazars, and the homes of the richer merchants.
Between this quarter and the ancient walls of
the city lies a vast suburb of ruins haunted by
beggars and pariah dogs, and beyond this crumbling brick barrier the Mesopotamian plain,—a
waste of tawny grass and white sand,—stretches
to a far horizon, broken only by the distant dome
marking the shrine of some desert saint.

In contrast to the empty ruins of the old
suburbs, the streets of the inhabited portion of
Bagdad present a singularly crowded and animated appearance. Even the principal thoroughfares are so narrow that two loaded donkeys find
it hard to pass when they meet, while the passage
of a file of camels on their way to the bazars
causes a veritable commotion among the itinerant
venders and petty merchants who make of every
doorway and open space a market for their wares.

In the street inhabited by the richest merchants of the town, it is almost possible to touch
with outstretched arms the houses on either side
of the way. As in most Oriental countries, the
dwellings present to the street sordid façades that
give little indication of the rank and condition

of their owners. The only windows giving on the public way are set high up in the wall, and are usually covered with heavy iron gratings that serve the double purpose of keeping out the thieves that infest the streets of Bagdad by night, and preventing the egress, unknown to the proprietor, of any of the inmates of the mansion. Often the dingy crowding walls on either side are corbelled out over the narrow way so that the projecting eaves of the flat roofs nearly meet overhead. Even at mid-day a cool twilight fills the whole street, while a promenade at night in the inky darkness of these alleyways, where the feeble light of your link-boy's torch falls on the huddled forms of scores of sturdy beggars sleeping in every sheltering doorway, and wolf-like pariah dogs sniff inquiringly at your heels, is not to be commended to persons of sensitive nerves.

In Bagdad the canine population enjoys privileges unknown even to the dogs of Constantinople, "the Paradise of Curs." It is an amusing sight to see a solemn merchant of the City of the Arabian Nights carefully picking his way around some sleeping mongrel who has confidingly stretched himself across the middle of the street for an all-day nap. Often you will see a small tent raised by the road-side to protect a lean bitch and her litter of yellow puppies from the rays of the sun. In a measure this is only justice, for, as in most Eastern cities, the dogs of Bagdad constitute the only street-cleaning brigade of the town.

Perhaps their most objectionable habit to the visitor unaccustomed to their presence, is their nightly chorus of defiance to the jackals that prowl about the walls of the city. At sundown as though at a given signal, from every quarter of the town and from the empty streets of the bazars, the dogs of Bagdad set up a barking staccato chorus. There is a moment's lull, and then from the far distance comes an unearthly concert rising and falling in one long weird note, the voice of the " wawi " among the ruins of the City of the Califs. And so throughout the night they call and answer each other, while you lie awake and listen, until like the old residents you grow to hear them no more.

During the cooler months of spring and winter, the population of Bagdad spends much of its time on the flat roofs of the houses. These

are only separated from the neighboring dwellings by low walls and wooden screens, but a
polite fiction, respected by every Bagdadi, has it
that nothing that goes on within the family circle
on one house-top is supposed to be visible to the
inhabitants of the next. Nevertheless, a certain
sociability is engendered by this life in common
under the blue sky, and the women and children,
to say nothing of the family cats and dogs, frequently go visiting from roof to roof across the
narrow streets.

The roof of our own residence was an especially favored spot, because from it we could look
directly down into the busiest part of the great
bazar. Here from sunrise to sunset the narrow
way was filled with a passing show—a kaleido-
scope of colors, costumes, and races, such as may
be seen nowhere but in the ancient Capital of the
Middle East.

The population of Bagdad wears in the
daily dress all the shades of the painter's palette.
Here one sees on every hand combinations of
color that in our climate would seem an outrage
against good taste, while under the dazzling flood
of Eastern sunshine they accord and harmonize

BAGDAD—AN OLD GATE

A STREET OF BAGDAD

in a way that fills the artist's soul with mingled emotions of despair and joy. For where is the Master who can do justice to these abbas and haiks of azure and silver, rose and violet, gray and green, toned to indescribable shades that only time and sun can combine?

In Bagdad it is only the rare European among the passing crowds whose costume appears awkward and inappropriate. Fortunately, however, while hordes of tourists visit Damascus every winter, and Cairo has become little more than a vast show for the entertainment of the patrons of the Messrs. Cook, Bagdad, encircled by its leagues of blazing desert, remains one of the few cities of the East where the street scenes are still free from the unæsthetic raiment of our European civilization.

Indeed, until a few years ago many European residents of Bagdad found it to their advantage to dress like the native Arabs, and the bazar merchant who would be bold enough to affect the ungraceful costume of the unbelievers would even to-day find himself an object of scorn and suspicion among his own countrymen.

The costume of a town Arab, which differs

considerably from that of the Arab peasantry, consists of a broad-sleeved cloak or abba of brown or gray worn over a long, tight under-coat of some bright color that stretches like a surplice to the wearer's heels. Around a tall red fez is usually wound a few strands of white cloth, that recall the great turbans still worn by the older generation and the more conservative priesthood. As in Persia, a green or blue turban denotes that the wearer claims to belong to the vast family of " seyids " or descendants of the Prophet, the only nobility of Islam. The slippers worn by the inhabitants of Bagdad also have their meaning, as certain colors and shapes are reserved for the Mohammedans, while the native Jews and Christians are obliged to content themselves with other specified shades.

The costume worn by the Christian women of Bagdad is especially striking and graceful. About their persons are wound yards and yards of light gauze netting—usually dyed in some crude but effective tint—slashed with tinsel and embroidered with gold, wrapped in complicated folds that cover them from head to foot in a blaze of color. Like their Mohammedan sisters, whose

costumes are of a sombre shade, the Christian
women hide their faces with a heavy veil or mask
as soon as they reach a marriageable age, and
this rule is usually followed even by the European
ladies visiting the city, to avoid inevitable com-
ment and insult.

The children of Bagdad, of both sexes, are
dressed in an exact miniature of the costume
worn by their parents. I can think of no more
dainty picture than that afforded by a little
Arab maid of from six to eight years, her slender
wrists loaded down with silver ornaments, her
bright eyes, ringed with dark cosmetic, and her
lips provokingly painted, like those of some tiny
courtesan. But, alas! her straight little nose is
usually disfigured by the heavy silver nose-ring
worn by most of the women of Bagdad, and
her face too often bears the cruel white scars of
the terrible " Bagdad boil."

This painful affliction, which disfigures the
faces of so many of the inhabitants of Mesopotamia, is supposed to be caused by the bite of
an insect indigenous to the date groves. The
running sores that ensue are usually confined to
the face, wrists, and other exposed parts of the

body, which would appear to bear out this contention. An inhabitant of these provinces is recognized all over the East by the deep white scars these sores leave behind. Needless to say, the fair tourists who occasionally visit Bagdad spend many anxious moments before their mirrors looking for the tell-tale red spot that denotes the first outbreak of the "boil"—and, most unfortunately, Europeans appear to be especially susceptible to this exotic plague.

A picturesque sight of the streets of Bagdad are the swaggering groups of desert Bedouins one meets on the occasion of some Arab pilgrimage. Armed to the teeth, chattering together at the top of their voices, keyed to the sandy wastes of their desert home, they pass you by with a scowl and a curse on the unbeliever. Their dark garments are powdered white with desert dust. Across the sand, under the pitiless sun, moving at a sharp trot, half hypnotized by the rhythm of some chant which drags them along faster than their sheikh on his white Nejd mare, I have frequently met them as they approached the city. With them they bring the sick or aged members of the tribe, slung between long poles carried on the shoulders of the younger men, the bearers with a dexterous turn relieving each other at short intervals, but never for a moment pausing in their swift pace. Arrived within the walls, their first duty is to visit the shrine they have come so far to see, probably the great mosque of Abd-el-Kader, who is a mighty Saint among the " desert dwellers." Here they pay their respects to a descendant of the Holy Man, who is still the guardian of his tomb. This personage, the degenerate offspring of his great ancestor, I frequently met driving in the suburbs of Bagdad in one of the rare European vehicles the town can boast of. He is said to believe with Omar Khayyám that the forbidden luxuries of the grape are after all the better part of existence, even for the grandson of a Saint. Nevertheless, his influence among the Bedouins remains unshaken, and he is able to keep up a handsome establishment near the mosque supported by the tribute of the poor pilgrims who visit the shrine.

Their devotions ended, the Bedouins wander through the streets, filled with childish astonishment at the wonders of the bazars. Laughing, unabashed, like naughty boys on a holiday, they press along, shoving the portly Arab merchants out of their way, handling the draperies and wares of the protesting shop-keepers, and finally end at the armorer's, where their last savings go for brass cartridges and ammunition. A trusty rifle and a good horse are priceless possessions in the "free desert," where there is no law but custom and every man's hand may be turned against his neighbor, if opportunity or caprice allow.

While there are many handsome horses to be seen about the streets of Bagdad, few can claim to belong to the pure desert strains. An Arab prizes breeding above all other points, and a horse whose descent from one of the great equine "families" can be proven with more or less certainty, will always command a larger price than a far handsomer steed of less aristocratic lineage. These "families" all claim to spring from the famous mare ridden by the Prophet, and her miraculous powers of speed and endurance are supposed to be shared by her descendants. Our kind host, the English Resident, was the fortunate possessor of a bay stallion of the pure Nejd strain which he had been allowed to purchase as a great favor from a friendly sheikh. Like all Arab horses he had the proud dancing gait, fiery eye, and plume-like tail of the " picture-book " steed, but it seemed to me that in general appearance he was far inferior to many of the horses to be seen in daily use about the streets of the city. The thoroughbred mares of these desert strains are almost impossible to obtain, and it is confidently asserted that none have ever been exported from Arabia, although this latter statement is open to doubt.

The Arab's affection for his horse, however, has not been exaggerated. Often you will see a Bedouin literally in rags bestriding a sleek and well-fed horse, whose condition has been its owner's first care. Arab horses are never " broken " according to Western standards. On the contrary, they are " handled " and gradually accustomed to their duties when still young, and in consequence most of them have very sweet tempers, and though high-spirited are rarely vicious. Unfortunately the cruel Arab bits ruin their delicate mouths at a very early age, and as an Arab is absolutely ignorant of the meaning of " hands," they all pull atrociously when bitted after the European fashion.

It is regrettable for many reasons that the Arab horse has gone out of fashion in Europe and America. While in point of speed he is far inferior to the English thoroughbred, trained for short swift bursts of speed on the turf or race track, over long distances, the pure-bred Arab is a magnificent performer and some of the journeys undertaken by the desert tribesmen are little less than marvellous. He has a wonderful faculty for keeping fat and in good condition on food and water that would ruin an ordinary horse in the course of a few days, and no amount of forcing will break his spirit and willingness to go.

Of late years a considerable demand has sprung up for small-sized Arabians to be used in England and India as polo ponies. Most of these are what are known as Gulf Arabs, and are far inferior to the better class of Arabian horses bred in the highlands of "Araby the blest." Recently, too, many of the best horses of Arabia have been forcibly taken by the Turks and sent to Constantinople, where the flower of the Sultan's cavalry are mounted on desert steeds.

The presence of the Turkish troops in the conquered provinces about Bagdad is as hateful

to the native Arabs, in spite of their common
faith, as to the Christian countries that still remain under the Sultan's yoke. The soldiers of
the Turkish garrison, in their unkempt European
uniforms, stained and creased by Eastern habits,
slouch about the streets of Bagdad with the air
of conquerors in a captured city. Just before
our arrival there had been a general loot of several quarters of the bazar by a mob of soldiers
whose wages had become the perquisite of some
superior officer. The Government, as far as we
could learn, never made any pretense of punish-
ing the guilty parties. Some days later, our
servant, returning home through the principal
street of the main bazar, was held up by a party
of troopers, who would have stripped him of all
his small stock of valuables had he not been able
to prove that he was in the service of Europeans.

I went one day for a stroll across the Bridge
of Boats that joins the banks of the river, to visit
the few monuments of ancient Bagdad that still
stand on the Western shore. Passing through a
mean quarter of half-ruined bazars, I came upon
a little palm grove surrounding the snow-white

Mosque of Sheikh Marouf, "a Friend of the Prophet." Scattered about the suburbs of Bagdad are the tombs of many fortunate people who during their lifetime were privileged to be the daily companions of Mohammed. No matter in how humble a capacity they may have served him, their names are revered by the faithful and their tombs have become places of pious pilgrimage. Even the Prophet's barber and his camel-driver have their shrines on the bank of the Tigris. And to be buried near the graves of these Holy Men is to secure for oneself their high protection for all time among the shady groves of the Mohammedan paradise.

The Mosque of Sheikh Marouf is surrounded by a little colony of marabouts and lesser saints who repose beneath square brick tombs, each one surmounted by a small white dome or cupola. Then in serried rank, crowding as near as possible about the dust of these chosen ones, stand the little white-gabled tombs of the faithful. Of course it is only the wealthy merchants of Bagdad who can afford the luxury of being buried in such company. The poor lie in miserable trenches in a dreary sun-bleached cemetery on the Mecca side of the town.

Not far from the Bridge of Boats stands what remains of the splendid monument erected by Harun-el-Rashid over the grave of the beautiful Zobeida, his favorite wife. Its tall dome of honeycomb vaulting is cracked, and tottering to ruin. The rich tile-work which once ornamented the octagonal base has been defaced and torn away, and even the monument covering the tomb itself has almost disappeared. Like hundreds of other noble buildings, these ruins have furnished the bricks from which the houses of modern Bagdad are built, and before long are doomed like them to disappear. The old green-turbaned seyid who has appointed himself guardian of the tomb hovered about us, dividing his anxiety for the " backshish " and his disgust at our profane presence in this lonely spot sacred to the departed glories of Islam. After we had rewarded him for his pious forbearance he directed us to another noteworthy shrine close at hand.

All about this building stretched an encampment of the desert Bedouins, their huts, built of reeds and hides, scattered at random over the plain. Among these rude shelters the camels, horses, and dogs of the tribe wandered at will, seeking such chance nourishment as they might pick up. Evidently, the custodians were feeling especially "hard up" that day, for at our approach the great wooden door was thrown wide open and we were invited to enter. We first passed through a large court-yard, for the accommodation of pilgrims, arranged like that of a caravansary, with deep, vaulted arcades or niches surrounding a central court-yard. In most of these families of Arab pilgrims were encamped, while in one an old gray-bearded mollah in horn spectacles was teaching a score of little Arab boys to read from the Koran. A copy of the sacred work stood on a small wooden stand in front of each pupil, and before these they sat on the bare ground, chanting the sonorous Arab at the top of their voices, bowing and swaying their bodies back and forth in time with the rhythm of the sacred text. Naturally we were objects of the liveliest interest to these youthful devotees, who turned in their places to follow our movements, never once, however, ceasing the monotonous drone of their task.

After removing our shoes at the door, we were allowed to enter the vaulted room contain-

THE TOMB OF ZOBEIDA

ing the tomb of the Saint. The rude coffin, made
of rough planks, which held the sacred dust, was
set on the bare pavement, but covered with an
elaborately-carved frame-work of cedar-wood,
over which were draped rich rugs and embroidered scarfs. On a wooden upright, at the head
of the coffin, hung a dusty and moth-eaten turban which may well have been worn at one time
by the deceased. The desert sun, beating down
on the brick walls of the shrine, made the heat in
the airless chamber almost unbearable and, our
curiosity soon satisfied, we returned with some
relief to the outer air.

At one time, all this quarter of Bagdad was
given over to the villas and gardens of the rich.
At the present day, however, the floods of the
Tigris submerge a great part of the surrounding
desert every year, and where once stood the
famous " Gardens of Delight," filled with the
wonders of the Arabian Nights, the hot white
sand of the desert drifts among shapeless mounds
of brick-work.

Everywhere among the palm groves that
line the banks of the Tigris one comes upon the
crumbling arches of old villas and palaces, with

the traces of splendid tile-work still clinging to them. Far out in the desert can be traced the dry beds of ancient canals which once watered spacious gardens and orchards, when the City of the Califs was the capital of more than half the world. The comprehensive scheme of irrigation then in use may still be traced among the desert sands for miles around, and it would require very little expenditure of money and labor to make many of these canals available for agricultural purposes to-day. The soil, in spite of the apparent barrenness of the region, is marvellously fertile, and in the neighborhood of Bagdad the Arabs are said to raise as many as three and even four crops of wheat in the same year.*

As one looks out across the white, glaring sands of the Mesopotamian desert, the stories of its ancient fertility seem almost incredible. Yet the long strip of fertile land lying between the Tigris and the Euphrates, irrigated by these never-failing streams, was known as the granary of the ancient world.

---

* The agricultural possibilities of Mesopotamia has been pointed out in an interesting pamphlet by Mr. David Fairchild, of the Department of Agriculture at Washington.

The only habitations one meets with to-
day are the villages of half-nomad Bedouin
Arabs, whose little fields of grain and scanty date
groves fringe the banks of the Tigris and the
Euphrates. Such agriculture as is carried on by
the Arab peasants depends on the same process
as is pictured on the old stone carvings of Nineveh—the wooden windlass made from the trunk
of a date palm, turned by a couple of oxen, that
draws a rude leathern bucket filled with water to
the level of the high river bank, where a primitive
device causes its contents to be emptied auto-
matically into shallow channels which distribute
it over the thirsty land. Such, however, is the
fertility of the soil of this "mid-river country"
that even by these primitive means the Arabs
manage to raise not only enough grain to supply
their own needs, but also carry on quite an important commerce in cereals with India, and other
ports of the Persian Gulf.

While the millions of India are decimated
every few years by famine, at their very doors
these golden harvests await the touch of industry.
The country between the Tigris and the Euphrates might become another Egypt under the

beneficient rule of some strong European power. Yet to-day it lies a burning desert beneath the yoke of Turkish misrule.

Bagdad owed its commercial importance in the past to its situation on the great caravan road across the Syrian desert, leading from the Mediterranean to the Persian Gulf. Since the beginning of history one great trading city after another has occupied this point of vantage. Within a few hundred miles of modern Bagdad lie the mounds that mark the ancient sites of Babylon and Nineveh, of Ur and Nippur, and other great cities whose very names are buried in the desert sands. Until the hardy Portuguese under Vasco da Gama had rounded the Cape of Good Hope, opening a sea-way to India and the farther East, the principal routes of communication between Europe and Asia lay overland. From the shores of the Mediterranean and the Black Sea a system of great caravan trails stretched eastward across the rich commercial empires of the Middle East, and from the volume of trade which passed by way of Bagdad, to the caravan road across the Syrian desert was given the proud title of "The Highway of the Nations."

The early history of these ancient pathways of war and commerce is lost in the mists of antiquity. Countless generations of travellers and laden beasts have marked them deep into the rocky floor of the mountain passes. Forgotten races have carved rude inscriptions on the rocks by the way-side. Some of these pathways may have seen the moving hordes of the Great Migrations, when the races of man passing out of the crowded homeland of Central Asia, travelled westward to settle the trackless forests and unpeopled wilds of Europe. Through long ages, where centuries count as days, while Egypt and Greece and Rome rose and fell in their turn, they saw the ebb and flow of conquest—the hosts of Darius Hystaspes, and the armies of Alexander on their way to change the destinies of the world. To control them became the key-note of Eastern policy even in the most ancient periods of history.

Later came the golden days of the Eastern Califate, when Bagdad, Ispahan and Bokhara, great trading cities of the Middle East, were names to charm with in the markets of Europe, and the merchants of Bruges and the Baltic sent their " ventures " overland by long caravans of camels to the shores of the Persian Gulf and the Indian Ocean, to barter them for the riches of Cathay and Araby. Persia was then one of the great commercial powers of the world, and the Seven Seas were alive with the sails of Arab merchantmen.

The traveller who passes along one of these old caravan roads to-day finds on every side the reminders of their importance in the past. Huge caravansaries built to accommodate armies of merchants and their beasts are given over to ruin and decay. The streams along the way are still crossed by the crumbling spans of ruined bridges, and in the midst of what are now desert places lie the ruins of once prosperous towns and cities.

Even in its present state of commercial decadence, Bagdad remains one of the richest cities of the Turkish Empire. To-day it is a great distributing station for European goods, which are eagerly bought by the Arabs in preference to native articles. From this point English and American manufactures are carried northward to Kurdistan and the Armenian provinces, eastward to the Persian border, and west and south into the deserts of Syria and Arabia, where the wild

NEAR BAGDAD—A CARAVAN

Bedouins wear robes of cotton woven in Manchester and carry repeating rifles brought from the United States. The exports consist of the products of the " desert " that lies about the city —grain, dates, and great quantities of the wild licorice-root that grows in the marshes of the Tigris and Euphrates. Rugs and carpets form another important item of Bagdad commerce, while from the fertile valleys of Kurdistan come bales of wool and goat's-hair, which are shipped to the mills of England and America. The Arabs and Kurds who inhabit these regions are a hardy and an industrious race, and the ancient cities of Diarbekir and Mosul are still important places in spite of centuries of Turkish oppression.

As early as 1766 Mesopotamia was looked upon as a promising field for European enterprise. At that time the " Turkish Company " of London dispatched its agents to look into the possibilities of opening once more the old routes of trade across the Levant to India. A few agencies or " factories " were established on the sea coast, and the foundations of British commercial supremacy were laid. In the early part of the century just closed a commission, acting for the

British Government, surveyed a line for a proposed railway along the Euphrates Valley, and pointed out the practical advantages of this route over all other overland connections between the Mediterranean and the British possessions in the East. The cost of building was estimated at about ten million sterling. As no serious engineering difficulties were discovered the road was actually commenced, but in the face of the opposition of the Powers interested in maintaining the integrity of the Sultan's dominions, and on account of the small prospect of any early financial return, it was abandoned after a few miles of rail had been laid.

A few years ago the English newspapers were filled with the accounts of another projected railway across Mesopotamia. The German Emperor's voyage to Jerusalem and the Levant, in 1898, left him fired with ambition to extend German influence, already strong at Constantinople, over the remaining rich Turkish provinces in Asia Minor. A German railway, operated in the interests of German trade, could serve this purpose better than any other means.

The idea of a railway from Hamburg or

Berlin passing, through "Greater Germany" (which to the Pan-Germanic mind includes Bavaria and the Austrian Empire) across Hungary, the Balkans and Turkey, to the shores of the Persian Gulf is a conception worthy of the Kaiser's imperial imagination and aside from the tremendous political effect of such an enterprise, like most of William's policies it has a sound commercial and practical side to commend it to the attention of his subjects. Indeed, the Bagdad Railway aims at nothing less than to reëstablish the ancient commercial highway which in the Middle Ages connected the shores of the Baltic with the great trading cities of the Levant and Persia, and laid the foundation for the commercial supremacy of the Hanseatic League.

It is fascinating to conjecture the effect this new line of railway may have upon the ancient centers of population it once more opens to communication with the world's affairs. Starting from Constantinople, and crossing the Bosporus by a great steel bridge (the designs for which have already been prepared by the German engineer Schneider under the patronage of the Emperor himself), the new Bagdad railway will follow the rails of the German-Anatolian Line from Haidar-Pasha, opposite Constantinople, to Eregli, about half the distance separating the capital from Bagdad. In a recent interview a director of the new company declares that work is to commence immediately on three sections of 200 kilometres each, only one of which, the section across the Taurus Mountains, presents any extraordinary engineering difficulties. The average cost of each of the three sections is estimated at ten million dollars. This tremendous sum the German company hopes to raise partly from the Turkish revenues and partly by capitalizing the rich oil and mineral concessions granted by the Sultan to the new enterprise.

From Hills, north of Aleppo the line will turn eastward across the desert, to a point near Birejik, where the Euphrates will be spanned by a long bridge of the latest design.* Continuing on through the oasis of Haran and Ras-el-Ain,

---

* The dreary desert between the Tigris and the Euphrates has been graphically described by a French traveller, Vicomte Maurice d'Orleans, to whose notes I am indebted for much of my information on the Bagdad Railway. See an article on "Les Chemins de la Perse," by Vicomte M. d'Orleans and W. P. Cresson, in the Paris *Illustration*, of August 29, 1908.

the road will then pass near Mardin, an important caravan center, until it reaches the more fertile country watered by the Tigris. Here a relatively prosperous region is crossed as far as the ancient town of Mosul, on the upper Tigris. Mosul is still an important manufacturing and trading city, and carries on an active commerce with Bagdad and lower Mesopotamia.

From Mosul the line follows the shores of the Tigris to Bagdad. Leaving this famous city, once the pride of Islam and the center of world civilization under the Califs, the railway turns southward towards the Euphrates, passing through the Holy Cities of Nejef and Kerbela, visited yearly by throngs of pilgrims from all parts of the Mohammedan world.

The next important stopping place is near Basra, whence the head-waters of the Persian Gulf are reached by steamer. To turn Basra into a river-port it would be necessary to dredge the Shat-el-Arab, the name given by the natives to the united streams of the Tigris and the Euphrates. As this would necessitate an enormous outlay of money and time, the German company hopes to obtain permission to continue the lines of railway as far as the little city of Kosima, in the bay of Koweyt, which the Arabs of the Persian Gulf use as a commercial and fishing port. Here the railway will come into communication with the line of steamers already plying the Persian Gulf, and in four days—with improved conditions of service—passengers will be landed in Bombay.

At the first glance it seems strange that a project so fraught with benefit to the commerce of the world should meet with active opposition from the Great Powers interested in the political and financial welfare of the Turkish Empire. The Turks themselves are anxious to see the building of the line pushed forward as quickly as possible. It was an easy matter for the German officers in command of the Sultan's troops to point out to their Moslem brethren the great strategical value of such a line. Instead of being obliged to maintain strong garrisons of troops in all the principal cities of Anatolia and Arabia, where the presence of the " trousered Turk " is looked upon with as much disfavor by the Moslem inhabitants as in the Christian provinces of Turkey in Europe, the Sultan would be enabled to keep them employed in guarding his Capital and person from the insults and aggressions of the "unbeliever." Another reason which appeals not only to the Turkish officials at Constantinople, but also to the piety of the whole Moslem world, is the important fact that the proposed road would form a connecting link with the Hedjaz Railway to Mecca, now in course of construction, which will change the long and perilous pilgrimage to the Sacred City of the Prophet into a pleasant excursion readily accomplished by any pious Mussulman who possesses the price of a ticket. This great work, which is to be the crowning glory of Abdul-Hamid's reign, is now being pushed towards completion with the funds furnished by faithful Mohammedans all over the Orient.

But the Kaiser has found that to persuade his "dear cousin" of Turkey is a far easier task than to secure the necessary coöperation of Great Britain, France, and Russia for a scheme primarily intended to forward German influence and commercial interests. In spite of an attempt to give an international aspect to the enterprise, the Emperor's efforts to enlist the sympathies of

Great Britain in the scheme met with dismal failure. His Majesty's Government with some reason insisted on regarding such a railway rather in the light of a menace to British prestige on the Persian Gulf, than as an advantage to her commerce in the Orient. Russia, on the other hand, sees in the wheat crop of Mesopotamia and Irak a menace to her own trade, and in the oil-fields of Kerkuk a rival to the productive fields of Baku and the Caucasus. Politically she has no more interest than Great Britain in seeing a powerful neighbor like Germany installed near her sphere of influence in the Middle East; moreover, her need of a German alliance in Middle Eastern affairs is past since she has come to an amicable understanding with the British Government as regards Persia.

It is known in Constantinople that the German Bank has only undertaken the management of this new railway enterprise at the Kaiser's request, not to say command. The most enthusiastic supporters of the scheme can claim for it but a limited measure of financial success for many years to come, and it would appear the building of the " Bagdad Bahn " depends on questions of political balance and interest which for the time being have been relegated to the background. But while little has been heard of the Bagdad line for some time, it is a mistake to believe that German influence in the Levant is not rapidly increasing year by year. The " Pan-Germanic " press has lately been making a great deal of the purchase by the Deutsche Bank of enough shares to give the control of the Anglo-French, Mersina-Adana Line, to the directors of the Anatolian Railway. This line can only be profitable as a feeder to the proposed prolongation of the Anatolian line towards the Persian Gulf, and the " deal " must come in the nature of a disagreeable surprise to the English politicians who believed the Bagdad Bahn to be what one of them gracefully termed " a pricked balloon." That the controlling shares were obtained by a clever trick from the reluctant directors of the Anglo-French Company, who now see themselves in imminent danger of being turned out to make room for a board composed of German financiers, can scarcely be comforting to those who have at heart the maintenance of the *status quo* in the Middle East.

X.

THE Holy City of Kerbela, the scene of the martyrdom of Husein and Abbas and other members of the Prophet Mohammed's family, lies near the Euphrates, about a day's journey across the desert from Bagdad. The Shiah pilgrims from Persia and beyond do not even visit the latter city, defiled by the rule of the Sunni Turks, but pass on their way to Kerbela by way of Kasemane, a small town built about a much-revered shrine, situated a short distance farther up the Tigris. In the eyes of a large portion of the Mohammedan world the pilgrimage to Kerbela is only a little less meritorious than a visit to Mecca itself. And while the " Haji " or pilgrimage to the city of the Prophet, may, in many cases, be dispensed with, a visit to the graves of his rightful successors is a religious and patriotic duty, insuring to the pilgrim the coveted title of " Kerbeli " and high honor in this world and the next.

Until within the last few years it would have been the height of folly for a party of " unbelievers " to attempt a visit to Kerbela without an escort of Turkish cavalry to guard against the fanaticism of the desert Bedouins. Even at the present time it is somewhat difficult to procure the necessary permission from the Turkish authorities, and we found ourselves obliged to await the pleasure of the pasha commanding the vilayet of Bagdad for almost a week, before the desired papers were issued. It was explained to us that this delay was necessary to make " proper arrangements for our safety," although our previous experiences had made me rather skeptical as to the real perils of travel in the neighborhood of Bagdad. At last, however, all the indispensable formalities having been observed, we were allowed to depart armed with a formidable document in Turkish addressed to the Governor of Kerbela, and a letter from our kind host, Major Melville, the British Resident in Bagdad, to the Native Agent who looks out for the welfare of the numerous pilgrims from British India.

To join the pilgrim caravan we were obliged to leave Bagdad before sunrise. In front of the Turkish guard-house on the western bank of the

Tigris we found awaiting our arrival a file of six or seven arabas, which comprise the daily post-caravan between Bagdad and Kerbela. An araba is a large wagon, with rudimentary springs and a canvas cover, capable of holding about twelve people, besides the Arab driver and the guard. Four small horses or mules are able to draw these lumbering vehicles at a fair rate of speed over the level floor of the desert, following the broad beaten track of the caravan road. Our wild Bedouin drivers in taking short cuts across country, over irrigating ditches and across the dry beds of old canals, frequently piled the unfortunate passengers in a promiscuous heap first at one end, then at the other, of the long seats; and time and again, as we watched their involuntary antics, we congratulated ourselves on having secured a whole vehicle for our personal use, in which we were, at least, able to brace ourselves by lying at full length along the seat.

Our faithful servant Abbas, dressed in his best clothes, his hair and beard freshly dyed to a coal black in honor of the occasion, shared the front seat with a Turkish trooper in a tattered uniform, armed with an old-fashioned Springfield rifle, which, from the date stamped upon it must have seen service in the American Civil War. The caravan of pilgrims who accompanied us was much larger than usual, on account of the presence of Europeans, and we learned that they looked to us for protection from the insults and violence of the desert Arabs.

Turkish rule in Mesopotamia, outside the walls of the garrison towns, often appears to be little more than a shadow. At rare intervals along the road we met a zaptieh or mounted policeman, one of those supposed to patrol the main roads and look out for the safety of travellers. In some of the larger villages a few Turkish soldiers were to be seen loafing about the bazars, and at every post-station we found a police-officer and a few guards. But so far as the desert Arabs are concerned, the Turkish authorities leave them free to settle their own disputes by the laws of blood-feud and the rule of their tribal sheikhs. Europeans and others travelling under Turkish protection, however, are fairly safe from molestation, as a swift and bloody vengeance is apt to follow any interference with the post service.

The appearance of the Arabs in the more distant towns and encampments was anything but reassuring. Almost every man we met was armed with a sword or rifle, and carried besides the traditional Bedouin club, a short stick with a heavy knob of black pitch fastened to the end. Even the little boys of eight or ten years stalked about armed to the teeth with miniature weapons, copied after those of their fathers. These " desert dwellers " are a tall, hardy-looking race, lean and prematurely aged by their rude life and lack of nourishing food.

Often as we passed one of their encampments of black tents the whole population would pour out upon us, the young men running along beside the carriages, shouting and brandishing their weapons and evidently enjoying the discomfort of the peaceable townsmen. There was probably no real danger of an attack, but our Turkish guard made a great display of preparing his ancient weapon whenever we approached a village, and I was not surprised to learn that highway robberies and even murders are not infrequent on the roads about Bagdad. The Persian pilgrims we met on the way were gathered in large parties for mutual protection. Often the caravans were headed by a man on horseback waving a flag attached to a long spear. These guides to the Holy City pretend to secure to their patrons safe conduct on the way. While on the march they chant in a loud voice their own bravery and the piety of their patrons, but I regret to say their reputation for courage is none of the best.

Soon after leaving Bagdad we found ourselves surrounded on all sides by the empty desert, where the only living creatures to be seen were " wawi " or jackals, who singly and in packs trotted leisurely away from the road-side as we drew near. Once we passed a group pulling and snarling about the remains of a camel, too much engrossed in their meal to pay any attention to our approach. Indeed, they appeared to differ very little in habits or appearance from the yellow curs we had seen a few hours before sleeping in heaps about the streets of Bagdad.

At sunrise the caravan halted and most of our fellow-travellers got down in the dust to say their morning prayers. Even Abbas joined in these devotions, and throughout the day we heard

him in scornful discussion with the Sunni soldiers
of the guard. As this was the first time I had
ever heard him enter into religious argument,
I set down his new-found zeal to the proximity
of the Holy City.

Several times during the day we stopped to
visit the way-side shrine of some desert Saint—
little brick buildings with whitewashed domes
and tiled doorways, usually set in a scanty grove
of palm trees. We had been advised not to attempt to enter any of these sacred enclosures,
although our fellow-travellers did not seem to
reverence them to any great extent, and only
paused to gossip a little with the venders of coffee
and dates, who sat in the shadow of their walls.
About noonday we crossed the broad Euphrates
(twin sister to the Tigris) by means of a bridge
of boats, at a picturesque village where buffaloes
and camels stood knee deep in the muddy stream.
Far up and down the river, the wooden irrigating-
machines filled the air with their shrill creaking
and groaning, and the Arab peasants were tilling
their little fields of wheat and barley. It was a
scene of patriarchal prosperity, probably unchanged since the days of Abraham.

KERBELA—THE GOVERNOR'S HOUSE

THE TOMB OF A DESERT SAINT

A PILGRIMAGE TO KERBELA

A little beyond this place we caught our first view of the great palm groves that surround Kerbela, with the distant gleam of the golden dome of the Mosque of Husein towering in their midst.

When we came to present our letters to the Consular Agent in Kerbela we had the misfortune to find him absent on a pilgrimage to Hilleh, and at first his servants seemed reluctant to let us enter his house. They even attempted to conduct us to a modest lodging in a distant quarter of the town, there to await the great man's coming. But knowing that in Eastern countries every man is likely to be taken at his own valuation, I insisted on being shown to the guest-rooms, threatening all manner of dire punishments in the name of the English officials in Bagdad if they refused. The effect was magical; their insolence quickly gave place to cringing obedience, and we found ourselves established in a large chamber among pink-silk curtains, carpets of brilliant aniline dye, empty bird-cages, and broken clocks,—in short, all the signs of modern Oriental comfort and luxury, with which the Nawab's house was furnished.

From a balcony before the house we looked down on a broad street leading to the shrines of Husein and Abbas. Although the hour was growing late the view of crowds of pilgrims and devotees hastening towards the sacred mosque decided us to visit what we might of the wonders of the city before nightfall. We moved abroad with some dignity, accompanied by an escort of four soldiers sent by the Governor under the command of a Circassian officer who spoke a few words of French and apparently acted as an official guide. On our way to the bazar he pointed out a large house in the center of a market-place which he declared the Governor desired to place at our disposal, and I could not but feel elated at the success of the stand I had taken, for, from being houseless, here we were with two " palaces " on our hands!

It was already dusk when we entered the narrow streets of the bazar that surrounds the shrine, and here and there little oil-lamps were gleaming in the dark stalls where the shopkeepers displayed their wares. Most of these are devoted to the sale of sacred relics, leaden tablets for the graves of the Faithful, symbolical brass ornaments to avert the Evil Eye, and the like. Another important industry is the baking of little tablets of clay, supposed to be brought from the holy enclosure surrounding the sepulchre of the Imams.

Many of the shop-keepers wore the white turbans of the priesthood, and some the green and blue head-pieces that proclaim the descendants of the Prophet. Most of them, while keeping a wary eye open for a possible customer, pretended to be absorbed in reading their Korans, bending and bowing before the sacred pages propped open on the ledge before their little booths, and droning out the sonorous Arabic phrases at the top of their voices, in the hope of attracting the attention of some pious patrons by this fervent display.

Among the brigands of the desert, and in the bazars of Persia where lying is practised as a fine art and an unvarnished tale is a thing of scorn, there is still one oath that binds men to the unaccustomed Truth. An Arab or Persian will swear away the salvation of his father and mother, and perjure the happiness of all his relations in Paradise for the sake of a few shahis,

but get him once to swear by the name of Abbas,
the martyred uncle of the Prophet, and you may
be sure his ingenuity is at an end—the truth is
out at last. For the Saint is quick to anger and
his punishment is swift on those who lightly take
his name. Yet here, at the very door of his
shrine, the poor pilgrim is fleeced with the same
impunity as everywhere else in the East. And
all their show of piety has not prevented the dis-
honesty of the merchants of Kerbela from becoming a proverb among their less crafty brethren in
Bagdad and Kasemane.

Our escort made a way for us through a
motley crowd of pilgrims from every land and
clime. Mollahs or Mohammedan priests, wild-
eyed darvishs and other Holy people far more
numerous than I had ever seen them before. As
we approached nearer the sacred portals, lowering glances were cast at us, and muttered curses
followed our progress. It was easy to see that
Europeans were an unusual sight in the Holy
City, and that their presence is looked upon as
an intrusion. Once or twice the crowd actually
attempted to bar our way, but the Governor's

soldiers shoved them aside with so little consideration that on several occasions I was forced to
interfere.

Suddenly the narrow street of the bazar,
along which we were slowly progressing, widened
into a little square, on the further side of which
rose a splendid gateway covered with elaborate
tile-work. Across this entrance hung a heavy
golden chain at a height so arranged that all who
pass in must of necessity reverently bow their
heads. Beyond the doorway we could see the
broad court-yard of the Mosque, flooded by the
level rays of the setting sun. A great crowd of
pilgrims filled this outer court, following the
chant of some invisible reader within the Mosque
with a thundering response. Standing in long
lines, their faces turned toward Mecca, they went
through the ritual of their creed, bowing and
prostrating themselves simultaneously to the
marble pavement: Afghans, Persians, Hindoos,
and Arabs standing side by side, their national
hatred forgotten for the time being in the fervor
of their devotions.

The crowd about us began to murmur at our
presence so near the sacred portals, and our guide

hurried us gently forward, following the line of the high wall that surrounds the double court of the Mosque. Once or twice as we passed through the bazar, we caught a glimpse, through an open doorway, of its mysterious interior, but never again were we allowed so close a view. Later we learned that a short time before our visit a Jew from Bagdad attempting to penetrate the interior of the Mosque in disguise, was discovered and massacred by a crowd of indignant devotees.

Only a few travellers have succeeded in entering the Mosques of Kerbela in disguise, and these only by actually taking their lives in their hands. The mosques are said to contain, besides the silver tombs of the Saints, splendid presents and rich gifts brought by generations of pious pilgrims. The jewelled swords of the great generals of Islam hang from the high domed roof, the highest tribute of heroes and warrior kings. Rich hangings, the finest product of the looms of Turkestan and Persia, are yearly brought in great numbers to ornament the shrine. The walls are painted and blazoned with verses and " suras " from the Koran, while the patterned

MOSQUE OF KERBELA

tile-work of the dome repeats again and again the names of Allah and his Prophet.

All day the thundering devotions of thousands of pilgrims who crowd the court-yards of the two sacred mosques are heard over the hum and bustle of the bazars. Late into the night, from our lodgings some distance away, we could hear the beating of tomtoms and the chanting of multitudes, and hourly until daybreak came the weird summons of the watchers in the tower, bidding the Faithful to arise and pray. " Allah-il-Allah! "—" There is no God but God, and Mahomet is the slave of God." The prayer that is first heard on the distant shores of the China Sea and following the sun from mosque to mosque across the countless leagues of Asia and Africa dies away at last on the Moroccan shores of the far Atlantic.

We were told that the next day a great festival in honor of some Saint held in high esteem by the desert Arabs would attract numbers of Bedouins to worship at the shrines. About midday we heard a loud tumult in the street below, and looking from our windows beheld a great company of white-robed Arabs passing at a quick trot towards the Mosque of Abbas. Every man was chanting at the top of his voice, many of them brandishing swords and clubs, and occasionally breaking into shrill war-cries. In the center of the advancing column an old seyid held aloft a tattered green banner, and about this ancient relic the pilgrims pushed and jostled for the honor of marching next their venerable leader. Their progress was regulated by the rhythm of their chant—sometimes a slow dancing walk, again a swift dash forward, before which the crowd of onlookers that filled the broad street would scatter and flee. Indeed, as we looked down on the sea of wild, upturned faces, tossing elf-locks, and brandished weapons, we were heartily glad that we had remained within the shelter of the Nawab's residence. Many of these fanatics, covered with sweat and desert dust, and excited to frenzy by their own dancing and shouting, presented a horrible spectacle. Some were apparently almost exhausted, while the old standard-bearer himself, lost in a trance, was borne forward, only held erect by the press of the throng about him.

This pilgrimage formed part of a great re-

ligious movement or " revival " which was agi-
tating the Arabs along the whole of the lower
Euphrates. At the time of our visit the movement was taking on a distinctly political tinge,
directed against the exactions of the Turkish
authorities. Indeed before we left Kerbela, from
the direction of Nejef came the news of a severe
clash between the desert Arabs and a strong
force of Turkish cavalry. The large number of
Persian pilgrims in town were thrown into a state
of wild excitement by this news, fearing a recur-
rence of the religious outbreaks and massacres
that occurred at Kerbela a few years ago, when
scores of Shiah pilgrims were massacred by
Sunni tribesmen, within the very shadow of the
golden dome. On this occasion, however, their
fears were not realized. This was fortunate for
us, as in disturbances of this kind the Arabs are
not discriminating, and an attack on a small
party of " Unbelievers " would attract less attention than in ordinary times.

We left Kerbela the third day after our
arrival, to visit the ruins of ancient Babylon,
situated a day's journey across the desert. On

account of the disturbed condition of the country around Kerbela, the Governor insisted that we should wait for an escort of cavalry, but as this could not be obtained without sending to Nejef, some distance away, we decided to start immediately under the protection of a couple of Turkish zaptiehs, mounted on diminutive donkeys. About midday we reached the banks of the Euphrates a little below Musseyib, at a point where the Turkish Government was erecting a huge dam or barrage across the mouth of a wide new channel which the fickle river had but recently chosen for itself in preference to its ancient course running somewhat to the eastward. At the time of our visit more than two-thirds of the volume of water flowed along this new bed, which had once been nothing more than an irrigating canal. This change threatened the prosperity of a whole province, and the Turkish Government, roused from its lethargy at the prospect of losing a large part of the tax-gatherer's revenue, was expending large sums of money and forced labor to turn the river back once more into its proper channel. This catastrophe which threatened to involve a whole province, including the country lying around the ruins of ancient Babylon, explains the way in which large and prosperous cities may be changed in a few years into squalid villages, and finally into the heaps of sand-covered ruins with which the Mesopotamian desert is covered to-day. Not long after our visit the worst fears of the Arab peasantry were realized, and the breaking of the Turkish barrage brought about the destruction of thousands of date palms and many cultivated fields.

From the barrage we continued our journey down the Euphrates in a barge employed in bringing brick from the ruins of ancient Babylon. We installed ourselves comfortably enough on the bottom of this craft, on a springy mattress of brush-wood covered with cocoa matting, while the half-naked Arab crew poled us down the shallow stream, occasionally varying this mode of progress by towing from the bank. On both sides of the river, the shores appeared quite fertile and prosperous. Numerous Arab villages nestled among the palm groves by the water-side, and as we approached these little centers of population we heard from afar the irrigating machines filling the air with their creaking and groaning. The villagers are said to rather enjoy these excruciating sounds, and an Arab proprietor would under no circumstances grease his water-wheels, as from his bench before the village coffee-house he can easily judge of his people's industry for miles around. We passed a troubled night on the boat, occasioned by our zealous escort, who several times fired his old musket at moving figures on the bank. He pretended that these were robbers, although just what mischief they could do to our party he was unable to explain.

Next morning found our little vessel anchored between the desert banks of the river, at a place once doubtless crowded with the shipping of ancient Babylon. Rising from the flat desert all about us were huge mounds of sand and débris that cover the palaces and temples of the Assyrian Capital, the last traces of one of the greatest cities the world has ever seen.

A few minutes' walk brought us to a well-built modern house standing in a small palm grove, and occupied by an Expedition sent out some years ago by the German Government to explore these interesting ruins. Here we were most hospitably received, and after an excellent breakfast set out to visit the ruins and excavations under the guidance of the learned Doctor Koldeway.

Of the place that once was Babylon there is little to be told. The Mother of Cities is but a name, a sermon on the vanity of human riches. Leaving the shelter of the little palm grove, we came out on a wind-swept desert—low mounds of gray sand, shaped by the desert storms, with the dust-devils playing between them—the site of the palaces and hanging gardens, the gigantic temples, busy marts, and other wonders of Nebuchadnezzar's Capital described by the writers of ancient days. Near by, the Eternal River still flows between desolate flats of salt marsh, white with rime.

Across the face of these mounds, and seaming the plain, were deep cuts and ditches where hundreds of desert Arabs, their hoods drawn across their faces as a protection from the driving sand, were at work with baskets and hoes clearing a way through the succeeding strata of débris with which town after town has overlaid the Assyrian city. A miniature railway was at work

in a deep cutting, where the court-yard of Nebuchadnezzar's palace is known to have stood, and
under the direction of blond-bearded, spectacled
savants in pith helmets, enough work was being
done to half finish the Panama Canal. All this,
that our modern curiosity as to how men lived
twenty centuries ago may be satisfied!

In the face of so much industry, it is sad
to relate that at the time of our visit the results
were somewhat meagre and disappointing. Compared with the remarkable " finds " at Nineveh
and Suse, the inscriptions and carvings found at
Babylon make a very poor showing. The ancient
city gives up her secrets reluctantly. A few
rudely-carved statues have been brought to light
—a curious lion carved out of black basalt, that
now gazes with vacant surprise across the empty
desert, and some broken shafts covered with
cuneiform writing, which were being prepared
for shipment to the museums at Berlin and
Constantinople.

The ancient inhabitants of the land were
probably too busy acquiring riches and power to
have devoted much of their time to the gentler
arts of civilization. But archæological research,

like gold-mining, is full of vicissitudes, and I was glad to hear that our enthusiastic hosts, shortly after our visit, made a " lucky strike," uncovering tons of Babylonian literature in the form of clay tablets.

On our way back to Bagdad the driver of the rough vehicle we had hired at a little village near the ruins told us a curious fact, which however I have not been able to substantiate. It would appear that a great part of the land covering the site of ancient Babylon now belongs to a rich Jew of Bagdad, who rents the land to the German " treasure-hunters." If this be the case, what a curious fate has overtaken the " Land of the Captivity," whose walls were cemented by the blood and tears of Hebrew captives so many centuries ago!

XI.

THE trip down the Tigris from Bagdad to Basra, where the Tigris becomes navigable for vessels of large tonnage, usually requires about five days; but taking into account the ever-present possibility of being stranded on a sand-bar, or on the muddy banks of the river, it is well to allow a day or two more for the journey. Our steamer, the " Mejediah," was one of several owned by an English company, who hold a concession allowing them to employ a limited number of boats in the river trade. As the volume of trade far exceeds the capacity of their steamers, each of these is obliged to tow a laden barge, carrying the surplus cargo, which adds considerably to the difficulties of navigation. Yet even with this handicap the English boats make better time than their Turkish competitors, and are preferred by the natives themselves.

For a long distance below Bagdad the scenery is extremely monotonous. The muddy Tigris runs between high crumbling banks of sand, which effectually shut out the view from the lower deck, but by climbing to the pilot-house I was able to look out over the gray desert with the " sand-devils " raised by the wind playing across its surface. At long intervals we would pass an Arab village, or the black tents of a tribe of desert Bedouins encamped on the shore, while scattered over the desert their lean flocks of camels, asses, and goats were cropping the almost invisible herbage.

Farther down the river, away from the protecting influence of the Turkish garrison, a rude mud fort, its walls pierced with loop-holes, and entered by a single low doorway, stood in the center of every village. The Arab population around Bagdad lives in a constant state of petty warfare, tribe fighting against tribe, and village against village, and these rude fortresses play an important part in the life of the community.

On board the " Mejediah " we heard many amusing stories of the " unwritten law " which govern these Arab " blood-feuds," of which the following struck me as an entertaining example. The sheikh of a small village near Bagdad, who had been living for many months in a state of desultory warfare with the head of a neighboring hamlet, at last hit upon a plan by which he hoped to bring their difference to a speedy and fortunate conclusion. From the captain of a passing river steamer he procured at great expense an old brass cannon, which he mounted near his mud fortress in a position commanding the stronghold of his adversary. But unluckily for the intentions of this desert Napoleon, the supply of projectiles he had procured with his piece of ordnance was limited to five or six rounds, and as his marksmanship was bad these were soon exhausted without appreciable results.

One morning, as he sat gazing sadly on his now useless purchase, aid came from an unexpected source in the shape of a flag of truce from the enemy with an offer, which to anyone who has not sounded the depths of Arab cupidity seems almost incredible. This was nothing less than a proposal to dig from the ground where they had fallen, and sell back to their original owner, the projectiles he had fired away and without which hostilities were for the time being suspended. After some parley a price was agreed upon and a regular arrangement made by which the merry war was carried on to the satisfaction of all parties concerned! What the final outcome of this peculiar condition of affairs may have been our informant was unable to state.

Below Amara we entered the marshes, where for the greater part of the year the Tigris runs in a narrow channel between low swampy banks. During the spring floods, however, the river broadens out into a wide lake, and the miserable Arabs are forced to flee to the high ground far in the interior, returning after the water subsides to cultivate the rich sediment carried down by the current from the valleys of Kurdistan and deposited on the sand. These marsh dwellers appear to belong to the lowest scale of humanity. The boys and younger men go about practically unclothed, while the women and girls wear only a long cotton shirt to hide their meager charms. As we passed near their villages the whole population would follow us along the banks, begging for oranges, sugar, and what they prize most of all, a box of matches or a little tobacco. For so isolated and miserable is the life these poor people lead that they prefer these trifling luxuries to presents of money, for which in their situation they could have but little use.

For many miles at a time the banks of the river would show no signs of human life or habitation, and our only diversions lay in watching the solemn pelicans as they sat fishing in long rows on the sand-bars, or an occasional shot at a wild boar rooting in the mud along the edge of the desert. Often on the lonely shores would appear mounds or tumuli marking the sites of ancient, forgotten cities, reminding us of the days when Mesopotamia was one of the great centers of the world's population. At Ctesiphon, we passed the ruins of the great arch or Apadana of Xerxes, a mammoth pile of crumbling masonry towering among the sand dunes that bury the ruins of two great cities—Ctesiphon and Seleucia.

The lower reaches of the river beyond the marshes grow less desolate in appearance. Near Kurnia, where the Tigris and Euphrates unite to form a single stream called the Shat-el-Arab, lies the traditional site of the Garden of Eden. Even in these days of scepticism the traveller must be hardened indeed who can gaze unmoved at the reputed cradle of the human race. The terrestrial paradise at the present day, however, is anything but a tempting place of residence. A

ARAB BOATS ON THE TIGRIS

ON THE TIGRIS—NEAR THE GARDEN OF EDEN

miserable village of mud huts, a Turkish custom-house, and a few scanty palm trees are the only attractions that it offers. The Tree of Knowl-edge is still pointed out, although if it ever bore fruit of the nature of apples it must have been a miracle, indeed, as it appears, in the course of time, to have become a species of stunted cedar.

A few miles below Kurnia we passed the reputed burial place of the prophet Ezra, a much-visited point of pilgrimage for Jews and Moham-medans alike. Many pilgrims were to be seen camped among the scattered palm groves that surround the shrine, and a fine new dome of blue tiles was in process of construction, to crown the tomb of the Saint. This, by the way, was the only building operation of any importance that we saw during our entire journey through Mesopotamia.

Basra, the famous seaport of Bagdad from which Sindbad the Sailor set forth on his won-derful voyages and whither he returned laden with the treasures of the East, is still a place of considerable importance. We approached the modern city, which is situated some distance from the ancient site, through groves of date palms stretching in a continuous band of verdure along both banks of the river. When the narrow screen of vegetation parted, we could see the country beyond stretching away barren and desolate to a far horizon; but from the river the feathery tree-tops made a welcome change from the desert scenery. The date crop forms the principal export of lower Mesopotamia and the ports of the Persian Gulf. These great plantations are looked after with care and considerable skill by their Arab owners, who during the date season camp out beneath the trees in order to keep a watchful guard over their crops. Dried dates are the principal food of most of the inhabitants of Arabia, and besides the enormous quantities consumed at home, many tons are sent annually to England and America. Basra is to-day the center of the date industry and this commerce, together with a flourishing export trade in wheat and an import trade in rice from Burma, makes it quite an important commercial center. Goods from Europe are transshiped here on their way to Bagdad, and as Basra has been spoken of as one of the terminal points for the Bagdad Railway, it may be said to be as near an approach to a "boom" as is compatible with its dignified age and history.

All we could see of the town from the river bank was a long line of sheds and "godowns" belonging to European firms who have their agencies here. Great piles of wheat protected by screens of matting were stacked on the bank, and women coolies were busily at work, standing knee deep in the golden grain. The American and English flags floated side by side from the high staffs of the consulates, near the Turkish custom-house, where a field battery of Krupp guns commands the busy harbor. It was an interesting sight,—in these days, when we are accustomed to hear our foreign trade lightly spoken of as a "political fiction,"—to see the Stars and Stripes floating over American commercial interests in this far-away corner of the world.

There still lingers an atmosphere of old-world romance about the trade of the Persian Gulf, which distinguishes it from commercial transactions in other parts of the world. One is constantly reminded of the days when the merchants of the great Indian companies of England and Holland sent their "ventures" to trade in these remote waters, returning laden with the spoils of the Golden East, or less happily to become themselves the victims of the manifold dangers that beset the navigators of the " Seven Seas." The native craft have high prows and sterns, carved windows and galleries, evidently copied from the Portuguese galleons which once sailed these waters. Many of the ships engaged in the Gulf trade have their sides painted with gun-ports in imitation of an old-fashioned man-of-war, and the steamers of the British India Company carry a rack of small-arms at the companion-way in case an emergency should arise. For even in these days piracy is far from being an unknown crime, as many a native trader becalmed too near the wild Arab coast has learned to his cost.

Our sailing was delayed by a not unusual occurrence, a sand-storm which raised clouds of prickly desert sand so thick about us that the captain could not make out his marks along the shore. We finally started, working our way cautiously down the river, past Mohammerah, at the mouth of the Karun River, from whose head-waters an important caravan track runs into

Persia; past Fao, where there is a Turkish light-
house and a station of the Indo-European cable
which binds Basra to the rest of the world, and
after plowing our way across the broad mud-bar
at the mouth of the Shat, found ourselves at last
steaming across the short blue waves of the
Persian Gulf.

Seen from the decks of the " Khandalla,"
the harbor of Bushire presented an animated and
a picturesque spectacle. A number of native
boats were anchored near the shore, and farther
out in the harbor lay the entire Persian Navy—
composed of one small gun-boat! This vessel,
purchased some years ago in Europe, is under
the command of a German seaman, who represents the several score of Persian Admirals and
other high naval officials we met at Teheran. At
the time of our visit to Bushire she was getting
ready for her annual trip to Bombay for supplies
and a new coat of paint, of which latter she stood
sorely in need.

Soon after our arrival six or seven large
native boats loaded with cotton put out from the
shore, and as they approached we could not but
admire the way in which their crews handled the

picturesque but cumbersome lateen-sails, stiffened with strips of bamboo, like those of a
Chinese junk. The boatmen of Bushire are a
mixed lot—Arabs from the " Pirate Coast " just
across the Gulf; brawny negroes from Somali-
land, and native Persians, the latter small but
well-formed men, clad in loose white shirts and
trousers. The operation of taking on cargo
began immediately with a great deal of noise and
clamor, which was soon augmented by the arrival
of a fleet of large row-boats, their crews sitting
on the thwarts facing inward and rowing with the
heart-shaped blades of their long sweeps almost
parallel with the thwarts. This appeared an ingenious way of shirking a hard pull, but later I
discovered that all boats on the Persian Gulf are
rowed in the same awkward manner.

On closer acquaintance, Bushire turned out
to be a substantial and thriving place, quite a contrast to most of the towns we had visited in
Northern Persia. The long-established trade
relations with Europe may in a measure account
for this, but it would also seem that the population is of a keener and more alert type than their
Northern brethren.

OUR CREW—NESTORIAN CHRISTIANS

Bushire is the center of British influence throughout Persia, the distributing point from which English goods are sent to every part of the Shah's dominions. It is, moreover, the chief port of the Southern provinces, and the terminus of the great caravan road leading northward through Shiraz, Ispahan, and Teheran. The British Resident is often called " the King of the Gulf," and in many respects this unofficial title is no empty misnomer, for besides the naval super-vision of the coast-line under Persian and Turk-ish rule, he is responsible for the good conduct of the petty sheikhs and chieftains of the " No-man's-land " of Arabia and the shores of Beluchistan.

With the tribes of that part of the Arabian shore still called by the suggestive title of the " Pirate Coast," England has come to an ar-rangement known as the " Trucial League." By the terms of this instrument these petty chieftains are bound to refer to the Resident at Bushire for arbitration, their differences with the Persian and Turkish populations of the opposite shore and the feuds that constantly arise among them-selves. Nor does the Resident hesitate to enforce his rulings by an appeal to armed force, and the appearance of a war-ship before the village of any recalcitrant member of the League soon follows any disobedience of his " suggestions." For some years past three or four small gun-boats of the British India Marine have been quite sufficient to keep the peace of the Gulf, and to give the necessary impression of British authority. Cargoes of " black ivory " may still occasionally pass through the straits from the African Coast, or an Arab blood-feud develop into a brisk little tribal war, but such events are looked upon as incidents hardly worth recording outside of private dispatches.

The Persian Gulf was the scene of many of the exploits of the famous Arabian traveller favorably known to us in our childhood under the name of " Sindbad the Sailor." In one of his seven eventful voyages from Basra he visited the Island of Bahrein, returning with a marvellous account of the wonders he saw there. Yet even his fertile imagination could hardly invent a story surpassing in interest the authentic history of these romantic " Isles of Pearl." Little do the wearers of this most lovely and fragile of

jewels know of the tragedies that often attend
its birth from the sea! What fierce eyes have
gloated over its beauties, and what crimes, even,
have stained its purity, before it is at last bound
about some fair white throat in distant " Farang-
histan "! For many famous pearls have a past
as dark and terrible as that of any enchantress
whose fatal charms figure in the pages of history
or romance.

The morning after our departure from
Bushire we sighted Bahrein, a long stretch of
low white sand-bank on the blue horizon of the
Gulf. The little town of Menama, the principal
port of this group of islands, is the chief center of
the pearl fisheries in the Persian Gulf, only
rivalled in the whole world by those off the coast
of Ceylon, and practically the whole population
is engaged in this perilous industry. The natives
of Bahrein are of the same race as the Bedouin
Arabs on the main-land, but from time immemorial they have followed the sea, living apart
under the rule of their own sheikhs, and many of
their manners and customs differ widely from
those of the Bedouin " desert dwellers."

The citizens of Menama are a wild and

turbulent lot, many of them the descendants of
Persian and Portuguese adventurers, for Bahrein
and its pearl-fisheries have been the first spoil of
every race of conquerors who have made themselves the masters of the Gulf. The town is surrounded by the ruins of Portuguese fortifications, and most of the little white houses are
solidly constructed, with loop-holed walls surmounted by military battlements, evidently built
with a view of impressing the fleets of Persian
pirates in the old days. Under British protection Bahrein has enjoyed many years of peaceful commerce. Yet it is doubtful if its Arab
population does not look back with longing to
the good old days when Might was Right, and the
laws that protect the Hindu money-lenders, to
whose share the greater part of the profits of the
pearl trade now fall, were not enforced by
British gun-boats.

We came to anchor about three-quarters of
a mile from the shore, and a number of native
boats set out from the harbor to convey passengers and cargo to the land. On the shelving
beach before the town lay a large fleet of small
boats belonging to the pearl-fishers. Most of

these were of the tonnage of European fishing-
smacks, built of wood brought from distant
India, for the barren coasts of Arabia furnish
little timber suitable for boat-building.

About a quarter of a mile from the beach
we came upon the astonishing spectacle of a
crowd of shouting donkey-boys and their meek
charges, apparently standing on some invisible
rock in the middle of the bay. As a matter of
fact, the shelf of coral of which the islands are
formed runs out for a considerable distance from
the beach, and at low tide these shallows are barely
covered by the receding water. To reach the land
dry-shod it is necessary to change from the har-
bor-boats to the backs of the waiting asses. These
handsome creatures celebrated throughout the
East for their size and strength, are usually white
in color, but the Arabs stain their coats with
henna in fantastic bars and patterns until they
resemble some new strange species of zebra.
Those we rode appeared to be almost amphibious
and carried us safely through the mazes of
broken coral-reef without a false step.

As we splashed our way towards the shore
the Arabs called our attention to a sight which

would no doubt have appealed to the imagination
of the much-maligned Sindbad. This was the
spectacle of a number of small boats anchored
a few hundred yards from the shore, the boatmen engaged in drawing fresh water from
springs at the bottom of the sea. These springs
well up strongly at a considerable depth, and the
entire water-supply of the town is obtained from
them. The fresh water is procured in two ways
—either in a goat-skin water-bag, which a diver
takes down with him and carefully closes before
bringing it to the surface, or by letting down
long hollow pipes of bamboo, weighted at the
lower end, through which the water rises up un-
contaminated to the surface.

The houses of Menama stand close to the
sea, between the sands of the shore and the sands
of the desert behind. We found the narrow
streets of the town almost deserted in the fierce
noonday heat; indeed, the only inhabitants we
saw were a company of beggars gathered beneath
the cool shade of a portico in the court-yard of a
snow-white mosque, the most prominent building
in the place. Near by stands the British post-
office, which is used not only by the inhabitants of

the " protected " islands of Bahrein, but also by
the Arab merchants of the neighboring towns on
the main-land, in preference to the entirely unre-
liable service afforded by the Turkish post.
There is also a hospital belonging to an American missionary society, which does a noble
work among the pearl-divers.   The records show
the greater number of cases treated to be
" shark-bite."

On returning on board the " Khandalla "
we found a number of Hindu pearl-brokers, who
were to be our fellow-passengers as far as Kur-
rachee.   Most of these belong to the Bunnia
caste, and come from the provinces of the Sindh.
Their dress consists of many folds of cotton
gauze wrapped about their bodies and legs, badly-
fitting coats of European cut, English patent-
leather pumps, and white cotton socks.   On their
well-oiled curls little skull-caps of embroidered
velvet hung precariously over one ear and gave
the finishing touch to a costume rakish in the
extreme.   On the forehead of each was a freshly-
painted Hindu caste-mark, an intricate pattern
daubed with white or red paint on their brown
skins, showing that they had properly performed

their devotions before embarking on the voyage.

It was strange to see the brawny Arab boat-man bowing and cringing before these frail, exotic personages. But the strength of these poor fishermen is no match for the wily brains that the caste system has developed through generations of traders. The Arab pearl-divers are usually in debt to them for boats and equipment, and often mortgage in their favor their profits for months in advance. It is these weakling traders who profit by all the toil and privation of the pearl-divers, for the price paid for pearls at the fishing-grounds is so small that it is more than quadrupled long before they reach a purchaser in Paris or London.

While the influence of Great Britain's " Gulf Policy " is all powerful on the islands of Bahrein, the Arab main-land is nominally at least under Turkish rule. All along the narrow strip of coast which stretches from Bahrein to the mouth of the Shat-el-Arab, the Turks have their garrisons in the principal towns and villages. They claim, indeed, to have established their rule over all the northeast portion of Arabia, but away from the coast their authority is no more

than a shadow, and the inland tribes own their
real allegiance to the Arab chieftain known as
the Amir of the Nejd, whose capital is Riad, in
the highlands of free Arabia, where the Turkish
armies have never been able to penetrate. Here
is found the real land of "Araby the Blest" where
the desert alternates with fertile valleys and
"wadys," giving pasture to countless herds of
sheep, camels, and goats. Here, too, are bred
the most celebrated strains of Arabian horses,
whose genealogy is proudly traced back to
the steed ridden by the Prophet. The few
travellers who have explored these remote regions
report the inhabitants to be industrious and con-
tented, living happily under the patriarchal rule
of their sheikhs as in the Golden Ages of Islam.
There are many large villages and towns, surrounded by fertile date groves and fields of
grain; but by far the larger part of the population, are nomad Bedouins—"desert dwellers,"
whose tents are pitched wherever water and
pasture for their flocks and herds are to be found.
Many of these only obey the desert laws of hospitality and revenge; but with a safe conduct
from some powerful chief, the traveller may pass

in safety from tribe to tribe, sharing each night their humble fare safe in the knowledge that his protectors must answer for his welfare with their own lives.

To the south of Bahrein lies the hideous desert of Southern Arabia, the Roba-el-Khali, or "Empty Abode." As a recent authority remarks: "We have better maps of the North Pole and the moon than of Southeastern Arabia. Never has it been crossed by any European traveller or entered except for a short distance by white explorers." Its only habitations are those of savage desert Arabs, miserable outcasts from the more fertile lands, who lead a nomadic existence, wandering from place to place by paths known to themselves alone. The Arabs of the Nejd tell with awe of whole caravans that have disappeared into its broad horizon, never to be heard from again, doubtless swallowed up by its merciless shifting sands. Yet at one time these deserts must have been the seat of an advanced civilization; fertile oasis and the ruins of great cities are said to exist far in the interior, and an occasional coin or piece of finely-wrought metal-work in the hands of the Bedouins often bears out this tale. The Roba-el-Khali has secrets which offer a tempting riddle to the explorer intrepid enough to face its perils.

Leaving Bahrein and crossing over once more to the Persian side of the Gulf, our next port of call was Bander Abbas. A much-travelled caravan route leads from this place to the interior of Persia, and it has been for centuries one of the most important commercial stations on the Gulf. The ruins that mark the site of the ancient city of Ormuz are still to be seen rising among the rocky pinnacles of a strange volcanic island which lies opposite the modern town of Bander Abbas. This city, founded early in the sixteenth century by the Portuguese, was one of the richest in the Orient, and over its splendors the priestly chroniclers of the time love to dwell. Its streets were crowded with merchants from every part of the Middle East. Its bazars were fragrant with the sweet odors of myrrh and the rarest spices of Cathay. So rich were the inhabitants of Ormuz that, we are told, " in their transactions gold was commoner than silver, and copper was unknown." Along a broad causeway, protected by towers and drawbridges, lead-

ing to the main-land, passed long caravans, bringing to the Portuguese garrison the riches of the
great commercial cities of Persia. In the harbors
of Ormuz the trading fleets of the Orient met
the galleons of Portugal and Castile, and even
junks from far-away China came to trade with
these adventurous merchants.

The Portuguese protected their town by a
great fortress built of hewn stone, whose ruins
are still to be seen crowning the heights of the
island. Near by are the remains of huge cisterns,
which once held the water-supply for the garrison. The failure of these during a siege caused
the capture and downfall of this commercial
Gibraltar when assailed by the combined forces
of the English and Persians.

The modern town of Bander Abbas lies
wholly on the main-land, its white houses built on
the seaward slope of a range of low ash-colored
hills, which rise between the sea and a high range
of mountains behind. The heat at Bander
Abbas is proverbial, even on the Gulf. Most of
the houses are surmounted by curious "wind
towers," with long slits or windows open on all
sides to catch every possible draft of air, and

without these contrivances residence at Bander Abbas would be intolerable. The inhabitants of the place are burnt almost as black as Africans by the fierce rays of the sun, and unlike most Persians, they wear as little clothing as possible. The agents of a couple of European firms and the British and Russian Consuls are the only foreigners to be found here, and their lot is far from being an enviable one.

Bander Abbas, in spite of its many drawbacks as a place of residence, is the center of jealousies and rivalries of the two great powers who seek to control the destinies of the Middle East. This is due to its position near the narrow Strait of Ormuz, which in war or peace gives it great strategic importance. Russia in the past has on more than one occasion sought to obtain exclusive rights at Bander Abbas, and establish a commercial port and naval rendezvous, while Great Britain, desiring to keep her predominant position in the Gulf, has intimated to the Shah's Government in no uncertain terms her determination to maintain the *status quo*.

Across the Strait of Ormuz, on the Arabian coast, lies the little Arab kingdom of Oman.

Throughout a hot, cloudless day we had been following the towering cliffs of the southern shore, when towards sunset the rocky wall was broken by a succession of gigantic clefts or fissures running down from its high summit into the sea. At the foot of each deep embrasure nestled a small village, and at the back of the deepest and narrowest of these natural harbors lay Muscat, the capital city of this desert principality.

Seen by the level rays of the setting sun Muscat appeared strange and unreal, like some dream city, such as the Lorrain would have delighted to picture on his canvas. In the ruddy glow, the iron rocks rising all about us flamed to a tawny orange-color, bathed by a sea of brightest cobalt blue. On a high ledge dominating the harbor stood a theatrical-looking little castle, with the red flag of Oman flying from its battlements, while at the back of the harbor the white houses of the town seemed to cling to the sides of the dark cliffs, as though at any moment they might fall like an avalanche into the waters of the bay.

MUSKAT—THE SULTAN'S STRONGHOLD

In the foreground of the picture lay the huge bulk of H. M. S. " Highflyer," towering above the tiny fortress and the rest of the shipping in the harbor until they looked like toys. As we came to anchor the Sultan of Muscat, who had been paying a visit to the Admiral on board, came over the side amidst a salute that sent the echoes booming round and round the rocky amphitheatre as he proceeded to the landing stage, while through a telescope we could see the flying banners of an opera-bouffe army drawn up in ranks to receive him.

Later in the evening we had ourselves paddled ashore, sitting on the dirty bottom of a gayly-painted native canoe, the Arab boatman keeping his frail craft right side up by sheer balance, much as though it were a bicycle. Our ignorance of native seamanship, and the close proximity of the sharp dorsal fins of a couple of hungry sharks feeding on the offal in the harbor, did not add to our enjoyment of the trip.

Near the landing place under the arches of an old Portuguese guard-house, we found a gathering of white-robed citizens enjoying the relative cool of the evening breezes. Muscat is built along the bed of a deep valley, and all through the day the high rocky walls concentrate and reflect the burning rays of the sun on the white houses of the town. Until long after nightfall the brick walls give off the accumulated heat, and this, together with the moist atmosphere, makes the sweating-room of a Turkish bath seem cool in comparison to the narrow shadeless streets. To the discomforts of the temperature must be added the indescribable smells of the native cookery, the sharp acrid smoke of the camel-dung fires, and the heavy reek of crowded humanity from the open doors of the little houses. Indeed it was not until, after our short walk, we lay panting in cane chairs beneath the hospitable verandas of the American Consulate, that we were able to draw a full breath into our lungs without feeling as though we were about to choke.

I afterwards learned that the heat of Muscat is famous even among the Arabs of the Persian Gulf. Succeeding travellers have quoted with feeling the description of the Persian poet Abd-el-Azels, who speaks of the climate of Muscat in the following terms: "The heat of Muscat is so intense that it burns the marrow in the bones.

The sword in its scabbard melts like wax, and the gems that adorn the handle of the dagger are reduced to coals." It is a matter of recorded fact that the thermometer often stands over one hundred degrees at midnight, so that few Europeans are able to support the temperature for any considerable length of time.

The population of the town goes about dressed in long loose robes of dingy white cotton, which seem in a measure to protect them from the heat, and the women, instead of wearing the gauze veils used in most Mohammedan countries, cover their faces with a curious black mask, embroidered with silver gilt, which gives them a decidedly carnivalesque appearance. The principal glory of the Muscat dandy is his short curved knife or dagger with its silver scabbard, and no matter how poor he may be this is the last article he can be induced to part with.

Next day about sunrise we set out in the cool of the morning to visit the town. Muscat still boasts of many interesting relics of the Portuguese occupation. Besides the picturesque castle which dominates the town, we were shown the remains of a large building bearing the

Portuguese arms, probably once used as a barrack, and the ruins of a Christian church. I also noticed several carved doorways, which appear to date from the same period, and in the Sultan's Palace we saw some fine old pieces of artillery bearing the arms of Portugal and Spain and inscriptions in Latin.

Near the entrance of this old building stood an empty cage where, until within recent years, it was the Sultan's custom to shut up thieves or other petty offenders in company with an Arabian lion. As the beast's claws and teeth had been filed away, the victim was usually more scared than hurt, but the spectacle never failed to draw crowds of onlookers to see this unusual form of punishment. Of late years, however, the British Government has used its influence to put a stop to this cruel diversion, and in consequence the cage stands empty.

Having exhausted the sights of Muscat, we passed out of the town through a gateway of the old Portuguese wall, and across a deep ditch, which has only recently been excavated as an additional protection against the Sultan's turbulent subjects.

Many of the houses in the town still bear
the marks of cannon-balls fired by the troops of
the Sultan from the old Portuguese cannon in
the citadel, when, a few years ago, he was besieged
by the desert Arabs. At that time they succeeded in capturing the town, and were only
persuaded to retire beyond its walls by the pay-
ment of a substantial ransom.

Within the shade of the old gateway a group
of the Sultan's picturesque troopers were loung-
ing at their ease. These were armed with every
kind of weapon from Lee-Metford repeating
rifles to Arab guns at least six feet long, with
carved, inlaid stocks, that would delight the heart
of a European or American collector. One old
fellow I noticed carried nothing but a spear and
a round shield, the weapons of the heroic days
of Islam.

Beyond the wall lies a large suburb of palm-
matting huts, built along the banks of a dried
stream or "wady." Here and there, wherever
enough earth has lodged in a cleft of the solid
rock to support vegetation, are a few miserable
gardens of vegetables and an occasional sickly-
looking palm tree. At the time of our visit even

these meager plantations seemed to be in imminent danger of disappearing before our eyes, for
the air was filled with what looked like a storm of
golden snow-flakes covering every branch and
blade of green. This turned out to be a gigantic
swarm of desert locusts, and the whole population of the suburbs was busily engaged beating
down the flying insects with sticks and branches,
stringing their catch on long fibers of palm leaf,
to be afterwards dried in the sun and eaten. So
esteemed are dried locusts among the Arabs that
the advent of such a swarm is hardly looked upon
in the light of a calamity. For a few coppers I
was able to buy a large quantity of this delicacy,
which in appearance and taste much resembles
the salted shrimps hawked about the streets of
every European sea-shore resort.

The entire water-supply of the town is still
obtained from the old wells dug by the Portuguese. These are strongly defended from the
attacks of the desert Bedouins by stone towers
and other fortifications. Patient little bullocks,
walking a weary round, draw up the precious
fluid by means of a primitive windlass, from a
considerable depth. These were the only four-

footed creatures, with the exception of a few miserable dogs and cats, that we saw during our stay at Muscat, and the reason became apparent when we learned that it was necessary, in view of the lack of other fodder, to feed these useful creatures on a diet of dried fish, a strange food which they soon learned to consume with relish.

The men of Oman have always been noted as hardy and intrepid mariners. From Muscat they have pushed their voyages along the coasts of India, and even to the distant shores of the Dark Continent. At one time the Imam of Muscat ruled the coasts of the Persian Gulf as far north as Bahrein, and held an outpost at Bander Abbas on the Persian shore. Many years ago the Omanese established a powerful colony on the Island of Zanzibar, near the African coast, and to this day members of the reigning family of Oman rule that place under the protection of the British Government.

THE END.

Milton Keynes UK
Ingram Content Group UK Ltd.
UKHW021339021123
431824UK00007B/112